Order this book from Amazon or from

Robert McFadden
139 Rosewood Circle
Bridgewater, VA 22812

Or rmcfadde@eagles.bridgewater.edu

ISBN-13: 978-1503269378 (CreateSpace-Assigned)
ISBN-10: 150326937X

COLLECTED WRITINGS ON
PACIFISM AND JUST WAR

DEDICATION

This book is dedicated to three of the outstanding professors at Manchester University (College) who influenced me while I was a student there, 1947-1951.

Dr. Gladys Muir was the first professor of Peace Studies, having started the program in 1948. She was my major professor; her vision of peace was supported by courses in the Philosophy of Peace, the Techniques and Procedures of Peacemaking, the United Nations, a broad Reading Course, and a basic Philosophy of Civilization course.

Dr. R. H. Miller was a professor of Philosophy and Religion. He introduced me to William Temple's book, Nature, Man and God. The book provided an intellectual basis for Christian theology.

The third was Dr. Andrew Cordier, at the time the Assistant to the Secretary-General of the United Nations, who spoke at the college on October 27th of 1950, during my senior year. He had been in the History Department at Manchester from 1926-1944. He was also the first chair of the Brethren Service Committee of the Church of the Brethren in 1941. His work at the United Nations stimulated the first essay that makes up this book, although written several years later.

The new director of the Peace Studies Institute is Dr. Katy Brown. She deserves recognition as she guides a new generation in peacemaking and reconciliation studies.

COLLECTED WRITINGS ON
PACIFISM AND JUST WAR

WAR AND PEACE IN THE NUCLEAR AGE

Robert McFadden

"When your children shall ask in time to come,

What mean these stones?

. . ye shall let (them) know. .

Joshua 4:21   KJV

CONTENTS

Dedication   Pg. 5

Foreword   Pg. 11

Acknowledgments   Pg. 15

Preface   Pg. 17

Introduction   Pg. 21

ESSAYS

Chapter 1   Perspective on Pacifism   Pg. 25

Chapter 2   The Nuclear Dilemma, with a Nod to Kierkegaard   Pg. 47

Chapter 3   The Pax Atomica   Pg. 79

Chapter 4   Paradox in the Nuclear Age   Pg. 101

Chapter 5   The Ethical Aspects of Limited War   Pg. 123

Chapter 6   The War in Nigeria   Pg. 153

Chapter 7   Nuclear Pacifism vs. Nuclear Realism   Pg. 161

FOREWORD

This is a historic collection of essays and I am thrilled to write this Foreword for it. "Historic" as a designation of this collection is no exaggeration. This collection represents the self-selected work of the first peace studies graduate in the history of higher education in the United States.

Many students and colleagues at Bridgewater College have known W. Robert McFadden especially for his award-winning advising and instruction in biblical studies, church history, ethics and logic. They also have known him for his direction of the College's convocation programs for thirty-five years and for which he likely has had more influence on more hours of liberal arts co-curricular programming than any other person in the history of Bridgewater College.

Dr. McFadden taught at Bridgewater College from 1961-1998 and became the first person to hold the title of "Anna B. Mow Endowed Professor and Chair of the Department of Philosophy and Religion." Many students and colleagues likely even knew of Anna B. Mow as an advocate of youth, peace, and interfaith understanding. During that time, he also administered the creation of a peace studies minor at the College and, through initiatives of the Kline-Bowman Endowment for Creative Peacebuilding at Bridgewater College, conversations are ongoing about the eventual creation of a peace studies major.

However, even persons who know Bob McFadden well may not be aware that he holds the distinction that the first paragraph of this Foreword mentioned (see the "acknowledgements" to this collection for more information). This collection of essays represents his biblical, theological, intellectual, and social journey. The reader will find Dr. McFadden to be a trustworthy guide through issues of non-resistance, pacifism, non-violence, and just-war theory, to the realism of Reinhold Niebuhr, nuclear pacifism, and considerations of peace in relation to the non-state violence and terrorism that have arisen in the Middle East and Africa since the start of the twenty-first century.

Dr. W. Robert McFadden has been my instructor, advisor, and mentor during my undergraduate study and major in philosophy and religion at Bridgewater College; my mentor and colleague when I joined the College's faculty in the department of philosophy and religion; and my friend. It is an honor to hold the endowed title and chair that originated with him. I have regarded him as a trustworthy guide for over thirty years and I am glad now to commend these writings and their guidance to you.

William E. Abshire, Ph.D.
The Anna B. Mow Endowed Professor
and Chair of the Department of
Philosophy and Religion
Bridgewater College
Bridgewater, Virginia
November 2014

ACKNOWLEDGEMENTS

Manchester University's recognition of my status as the first Peace Studies major came about in part because my brother, Wilbur, worked with Dr. Katy Brown, chair of the Peace Studies Institute, to acknowledge the fact. There had been some confusion because in 1951 there was one major and two minors in the department. The program had been started in 1948 and some early records were not clear even though the information was known. Wilbur has also urged me to publish some of my writings on war and peace, and has been an "advocate" for their relevance and value.

At the ceremony in the Peace Garden on Homecoming, October 11, 2014, I told both of them that perhaps my major contribution to peace studies since I had graduated was my writings. My essays and articles had appeared in various journals and magazines over the years. I have brought them together here so that they are accessible in one place. They certainly represent a cross section of the changes in my thinking.

As was true in the first book of essays I had published, my brother Ralph has encouraged me to tackle the project. Indeed, he has volunteered to do the editing and submission of the material to the printer! Without his encouragement and assistance, this book would not have come to fruition. My special friend, Glenna Wampler, has also given me encouragement and support.

The biblical quotation is from the KJV of the Bible.

PREFACE

The first essay, "Perspective in Pacifism," first appeared the journal, Brethren Life and Thought, 6, No. 2 (Spring, 1961), 36-52. It is reprinted here with permission. It has stood the test of time. The three types of pacifism described and documented (nonresistance, nonviolence, and vocational pacifism) still dominate the thought of the Church of the Brethren and the Brethren Revival Fellowship. The Brethren Revival Fellowship refers to "nonviolence" as "secular pacifism." It appears to me that the concept of "vocational pacifism" is accepted by many in the Church of the Brethren today. "Nonviolence" is accepted ecumenically.

The second essay first appeared in the journal, Theology Today, which is published by Princeton Theological Seminary. The essay was published as "The Nuclear Dilemma, with a Nod to Soren Kierkegaard," Vol. 17, No. 4 (January, 1961), 505-518. It also has stood the test of time. What was said about nuclear pacifism, about Abraham's sacrifice of Isaac, and about Soren Kierkegaard, are all still true today. Most importantly, the article called for a new spiritual discipline not to use nuclear weapons. That is still holding nearly seventy years after

Hiroshima! The nuclear weapons were possessed but not used during the Cold War.

The third essay, "The Pax Atomica," was first published in the journal, Brethren Life and Thought, Vol. 32, (Winter, 1987), 45-52. It deals with background issues in any discussion about the nuclear dilemma and the abolition of war in the future.

A fourth essay, "Paradox in the Nuclear Age," appeared in the Manchester University Bulletin of the Peace Studies Institute, 14 (1984), 12-18. The article describes the issues and tensions between the nuclear pacifists and the nuclear realists. The paradox arises in the moral response to thermonuclear weapons, whether to possess them or to renounce them. The "better red than dead" position was countered by those who said, "better dead than red". The two positions in the debate were countered by most theorists who offered an alternative, "Better neither Red nor Dead," and argued to possess the weapons, but hoped that they would not use them.

The fifth essay in the book was first given as a lecture on a panel at the Institute on Limited War at the State College of Arkansas, Conway, Arkansas. The lecture was later printed in the Journal of Church and State published in Waco, Texas: "The Ethical Aspects of Limited War,"

13 (Winter, 1971), 113-127. It is reprinted here with permission. It was one of three lectures given at the Institute, the other two being "The Military Aspects of Limited War" and "The Political Aspects of Limited War." I tried to answer the questions in my lecture, When is war right? And What is right in war?

The sixth essay is the most recently written. It was published in my book, Is the Bible Correct?, in 2013. I am printing it again here because it is part of my thinking about war and peace. It also reflects recent developments that demand renewed discussion in the Church of the Brethren about our responses to war. It also reflects my own thinking about the relevance of the just war tradition to the continued problems faced by the Christian Church. The crusade of the Islamic Terrorists who want to establish a "Sharia" state appears to be a problem that will persist for many years, not only in Nigeria but in many areas of the globe.

The last "essay" was a talk that I gave to my Bridgewater Rotary Club on August 6, 2013. It called attention to the anniversary of the bombing of Hiroshima on that date in 1945. I then went on to describe the writing of my dissertation on Nuclear Pacifism vs. Nuclear Realism. Attached to this talk are the arguments of the nuclear pacifists and the nuclear realists. They represent the core of the dissertation. I have used them in classes and other teaching situations. The arguments are still valid today in representing the two positions in the larger ecumenical Christian Church.

INTRODUCTION

On October 11, 2014, at a ceremony that was part of Manchester University's Homecoming, I was presented with a certificate acknowledging that I was the first MU graduate to major in Peace Studies. That was in 1951, three years after Dr. Gladdys Muir had initiated the Peace Studies program in 1948. When reflecting upon that recognition, I told my brother Wilbur and Dr. Katy Brown that I thought my contribution to "Peace Studies" in the years that followed was in my writings. I knew that most of those writings had appeared in journals and periodicals, and I decided to bring them together in a book where they would be more easily accessible.

I had been interested in questions regarding war and peace for many, many years. I grew up in a parsonage; my father was a pacifist during World War II. In his congregation, he kept in contact with those young men who had gone into Civilian Public Service and those who had gone into the Armed Forces. I learned the theology and the practice of being a pacifist. The first newspaper headline I remember was "Germany Invades Poland" on September 1, 1939. I bought Church of the Brethren Peace Certificates rather than US War Stamps. The first article that I wrote that was published in the local newspaper was about "war atrocities." It appeared in 1946-1947, my senior year in high school.

Majoring in Peace Studies at Manchester was a natural fit for my interests and questions. Although I did not know it at the time, another course at Manchester had a profound influence on me. Dr. R. H. Miller taught a course on the philosophy of religion. He used as a text the book by William Temple, Nature, Man and God. It was a basic course in Christian Theology. It served as a foundational text in my theological education at seminary.

Some of the term papers that I wrote in seminary and graduate school arose out of my interest in questions of war and peace. Although my major in graduate school was systematic theology, I ended up doing my dissertation on a social ethics issue, Nuclear Pacifism vs. Nuclear Realism. Despite my background and training in the best of pacifism, I ended up being a nuclear realist, following in the tradition of just war theory, resulting from my dissertation studies.

During the second year that I taught at Juniata College, (1956-1957, Second Semester), before I went to Boston for graduate school, I taught a new course approved by the faculty on the Theology of Peace. The theology that was the basis of the course was the thinking of well-known Christian theologians, both Protestant and Roman Catholic. My reading of Reinhold Niebuhr and other theologians led me in the direction of just war theory.

My church activities also contributed to my interest in international relations and war/peace questions. During my senior year in high school, I attended the first Church of the Brethren' Citizen Youth Seminar in Washington, D.C. in the spring of 1947.

In my last year in college, I was a denominational youth delegate to the Constituting Convention of the National Council of Churches held in Cleveland, Ohio. It was from November 28th to December 1st, 1950. During the Conference, the Chinese entered the Korean War, and I heard major addresses about how the churches should respond to the crisis. I was deeply impressed.

A turning point in my thinking had occurred during a convocation at Manchester College earlier in the fall. Andrew Cordier, assistant to the secretary-general of the United Nations spoke at a college chapel. He described his role in the UN in responding to North Korean invasion of South Korea in the summer of 1950. He said that the United Nations responded with social, economic and political means as well as military force. Andrew Cordier was an ordained minister in the Church of the Brethren. He had been the chair of the Brethren Service Committee in 1940-41. He was chair of the History department at Manchester College before joining the State Department, and eventually the United Nations staff. I still regard him as the greatest international civil servant ever to come out of the Church of the Brethren.

Perspective in Pacifism

It has been twenty years since my mind was first confronted consciously with the conflict and tension existing in the Christian conscience concerning war and peace. My thinking has been initially cradled and nurtured in the Church of the Brethren. And it is not only appropriate, but also in a sense of gratitude to the many who have taught me, that I now seek to clarify some of the conflicting concepts of pacifism which seem to me to be advocated in our denomination. It is my hope that in so doing we may be better servants of the Word in our teaching and ministering. For this reason the following typology is submitted to the readers of *Brethren Life and Thought*. The three categories which are described imply widely differing foundations and have conflicting implications. They stem from contrasting theological positions and lead to differing results in church discipline, political action, and human relationships.

When the Korean War broke out in the summer of 1950, our church offices in Elgin sent out a memo sharing with us some of their own thinking regarding the Brethren and that war. We became aware again of our historic peace witness and its incompatibility with the use of force and violence which had erupted at the 38th parallel. In the fall of that same year, Andrew Cordier of the United Nations, an ordained minister in the Church of the Brethren, spoke to the Manchester College community concerning the role of the United Nations in the Korean crisis.[1] In so doing he revealed his own involvement and responsibility in assembling the UN police force in Korea. What this Brethren minister was *doing* was quite in contrast to what other Brethren ministers were *saying.*

In other words, by example and by teaching we are presenting a confused picture to our young people. The answer is *not* conformity, but neither can we continue to broadcast an anarchy of ideas about one of our chief concerns. We need to rethink and to reconsider our attitude toward war and peace in our age, and in doing so use the resources of the entire Christian church and Christian tradition and not only our own peculiar heritage. We must learn to think and to wrestle with our fellow Christians in this area of concern as well as in other areas. We have assumed too long that we, the "pacifists," have been right and they, the "non-pacifists," have been wrong. Actually all of us are faced with a new historical situation and we must learn from each other if we are going to meet adequately the crisis in which

God confronts us.

A. Nonresistance

It should be generally recognized that the background of the thinking of the Brethren is rooted in a philosophy of nonresistance which stems from our Anabaptist heritage. And yet it is true that this will sound unfamiliar to many youth of the present generation. The Brethren have changed their outlook and perspective. However much we maintain that we are a "historic peace church" we must acknowledge that our philosophy about the Christian and war has undergone certain changes, especially in the twentieth century.

From the beginning of the quiet phase of the Anabaptist movement an emphasis was placed on nonresistance as the Christian response to evil. One of the earliest representative statements can be taken from a sermon by Hans Marquardt, a minister of the Swiss Brethren, which he preached at St. Gall, Switzerland, in 1528.

> "We confess that civil government is necessary and is a divine appointment and that the use of the sword by the government is good and

necessary, and we say with Paul, Rom. 13, that every man should be subject and obedient to the higher power, not only to a mild and peaceful but also a tyrannical government, for the reason that there is no power but of God. Therefore all believers, under whatever government they may live, will not complain of heavy burdens, nor will they resist the government or cause trouble or uproar on account of what they may be called upon to bear. In matters of their faith, however, the believers are responsible to God alone to whom they owe greater obedience than to man. Therefore all our brethren esteem their faith in God through Christ Jesus, our Saviour, as the highest, greatest and most valuable thing, and of this we do not suffer ourselves to be robbed even if our life is at stake. But in matters which do not concern faith and conscience and do not conflict with our duty to God, we are ready to obey the civil government in anything that may be asked of us. And if the government, contrary to justice and right, confiscates our property and reduces us to poverty, we bear and suffer it, since it is impossible for us to escape such oppression without transgression and disturbance. But that the Christian should be an executive of the government, or a magistrate, we do not admit. Christ says, Luke 22, "The kings of the gentiles exercise lordship over them and they that exercise authority upon them are called benefactors. But among you it shall not be so, but he that is greatest among you, let him be as the younger; and he that is chief as he that doth serve." Here the believers are forbidden the execution of government by force. And the fact that under the Old Covenant God has permitted His people the use of the sword does not concern us or bind us, for the old law has been replaced by the new commandment of Christ that we should love our enemies .... The believer is not to be an earthly ruler, or to use violence, or to go to war, or use the sword."[2]

Writings by Menno Simons reflect the same depth of conviction and the same perspective on the relation of church and state.

"My dear reader, if the poor, ignorant world with an honest heart accepted this our hated and despised doctrine, which is not of us but of Christ, and faithfully obeyed it, they could well change their deadly swords into plow-shares and their spears into pruning hooks, level their gates and walls, dismiss their executioners and henchmen. For all who accept our doctrine in its power, will by God's grace not have any ill will to anyone upon earth, and not against their most bitter enemies, much less wrong and harm them by deeds and actions; for they are children of the Most High who from their hearts love that which is good and in their weakness avoid that which is evil; nay, hate it and are inimical thereto." (II:I03a).[3]

What is involved is not only a doctrine of nonresistance to evil, but also a doctrine of the state which allows the Christian to sanction the state's use of force but does not allow the Christian himself to have any part in that use of force. Umphrey Lee is right when he says, "The general attitude ... was that of withdrawal from the world, although there were differences between groups as to the extent of this withdrawal."[4]

All of the evidence indicates that the early Brethren, even though their founding was two hundred years after the beginning of Anabaptism, adhered to the doctrine of nonresistance. Rufus Bowman cites the minutes of Annual Conference of 1785 as the earliest available statement of the church which upheld nonresistance. After quoting relevant Scripture passages, the Annual Conference stated:

"So we hope the dear Brethren will not take it amiss when we, from all these passages of Scripture, and especially from the words of Peter, cannot see or find any liberty to use any (carnal) sword, but only the sword of the Spirit, which is the word of God..

"But that the higher powers bear the sword of justice, punishing the evil and protecting the good, in this we acknowledge them from the heart as the ministers of God. But the sword belongeth to the kingdom of the world, and Christ says to his disciples: "I have chosen you from the world," etc. Thus we understand the beloved Peter, that we are to submit ourselves in all things that are not contrary to the will or command of God, and no further."[5]

Dr. Bowman adds, "There is no evidence that this is a change of the church's original position. We may assume rather that it is an expression of it."[6] And this position characterized the Brethren through the decade of the 1920's. In the Annual Conference resolutions of 1924, this statement is made: "All the teachings and precepts of our Lord on the subject of non-resistance in personal conduct or in attitude towards militant service were exemplified by him in his contact with men and authorities."[7]

Some of the presuppositions of non-resistance would appear to be the following:

1. God calls us always to bear suffering rather than inflict suffering.
2. Christ intends that we accept literalistically the teachings concerning nonresistance in the Sermon on the Mount.
3. While government and its use of power and force are ordained of God, the Christian is called to witness to a way of perfect love.
4. The wrath of God is an Old Testament concept; we are called to live according to the dictate of the New Testament,

which is love.

5. The taking of human life is always and under all circumstances contrary to the will of God.

B. Nonviolence

Arising out of the religious thought of the East and being modified by outstanding Christians, the idea of nonviolence became a vital part of the social gospel movement in this country during the early part of the twentieth century. The movement for independence in India led by Mahatma Gandhi and the activities of the Fellowship of Reconciliation to build peace following World War I added to the impact of the crusade within the American church to recognize nonviolent resistance as the most adequate Christian approach to the world's ills.

The philosophy back of the use of nonviolence is significantly different from that of nonresistance. The latter decries the use of any coercion; the former uses coercion in nonviolent forms to achieve desired goals. Yet both are similar in their effort to interpret the teachings of Jesus more forcefully and in their understanding of overcoming evil with good.

The initial impact of the philosophy of nonviolence on Brethren thought became evident during the decade of the 1930's. In 1932, in a special Annual Conference resolution, a change in attitude toward the state became apparent.

> "We feel bound to avow our conviction that all war is out of harmony with the plain precepts of the Gospel of Christ, and that no plea of necessity or policy, however urgent, can be set up to release either the individual or any nation from the paramount duty which they owe to Jesus who enjoined all men to love their enemies."[8]

The separation of the spheres of government and church is no longer recognized. As the Brethren came out from under their sectarian shelter, they desired to become more involved in the problems of the world. The social gospel movement in its aspect of a nonviolent approach to international conflict appealed to us.

In the historic statement of the Annual Conference of 1935 the explicit turning from "nonresistance" to "nonviolence" is carried through. The key sentence for our understanding of the philosophy gaining ascendancy in the Church of the Brethren may be quoted as follows: "We believe that non-violence, motivated by goodwill, is more powerful than the sword, making possible the survival of both parties, while warfare insures the ultimate destruction of both."[9] And later in the same resolution is added, "We believe in the only preparedness for our nation - goodwill, and the agencies through which it may be expressed and maintained."[10]

Debate between "social gospel liberalism" and "Niebuhrian neo-orthodoxy" dominated the pages of the *Christian Century* during this period. A lead article by Kirby Page in the January 9, 1935,[11] issue of this periodical, "If War Is Sin," may have influenced those who drew up the resolutions for Annual Conference in 1935. It was only twelve months earlier that Reinhold Niebuhr had written an article, "Why I Leave the F. O. R." There he wrote:

"In so far as we are radical Christians we must find a more solid ground for the combination of radicalism and Christianity than the creed of pacifism supplied. But we will always maintain our respect for the purity of purpose which animates the men who conceived the Fellowship of Reconciliation and will carry it on in spite of discouragement in these critical days. Perhaps the day will come when we will be grateful for their counsels."[12]

And on reflection, Paul Tillich in 1949 added a note of perspective to the debate of the thirties.

"While in my first years in the United States I was surprised and worried by the tremendous emphasis put on the question of pacifism - a question that seemed to me of minor importance and often the result of confused thinking. I presently discovered that all theological problems were implicit in this problem. When, therefore, in the years before, during and after the Second World War, the pacifist ideology was shattered in large numbers of people I understood that this was an indication of a new attitude toward the doctrine of man and toward the whole of Christianity. And this change in the mind of others made it easier for me to feel at home in the theological work of this country."[13]

Much of the leadership in the Church of the

Brethren aligned itself with the nonviolent philosophy in the debate which symbolized the change from liberalism to neo-orthodoxy in theology in leading American seminaries. That is not to say that the Brethren were characterized in other ways by a theology of liberalism; we maintained a conservative understanding of sin and salvation and a fundamentalistic outlook on certain New Testament teachings. But our definite liberal stand on pacifism made it difficult to classify the theology of the brethren in any of the more recognized schools of thought. We sought to maintain our peace witness, in which we were assimilating the philosophy of nonviolence, and at the same time enter seriously into ecumenical discussion; it was a difficult task.

Despite the fact that the philosophy of nonviolence fell into disrepute in certain schools of theological thought, it continued to be recognized as a potent force for good on the world scene. Especially in the United States has it proved its validity in the complex social revolution marking the change from segregation to integration. Martin Luther King, Jr., has made the nonviolent method of love the only really desirable approach to effect the Negroes' rights and goals.[14]

Some of the presuppositions of the philosophy of nonviolence may be stated as follows:

1. The Christian has a responsible role to play in the life of the nations and in the functions of government.
2. Nonviolent coercion is the approach that Christ would take to bring about social change; the use of violence is contrary to his mind and spirit.
3. This way of love is imperative for the Christian and in the long perspective of history achieves victory over evil.
4. It is more adequately possible through the means of nonviolence to express the command to love while working to overcome evil.
5. Christ was active and revolutionary in his attack on the personal and social evils of his day.

C. Vocational Pacifism

Although the most effective challenge to pacifism in this country came from the pen of Reinhold Niebuhr,[15] it was also Dr. Niebuhr who saw the value and place for a minority witness in the life of the church.

"The attempt to maintain an absolute Christian ethic against the relativities of politics, essentially the strategy of the Christian ascetics, is a valuable contribution to Christian thought and life. We ought to have not only the symbol of the Cross, but recurring historical symbols of the tension between the Christian ideal and the relativities and compromises in which we are all involved .... Religious pacifism, as a part of a general ascetic and symbolic portrayal of love absolutism in a sinful world, has its own value and justification. A Church which does not generate it is the poorer for its lack."[16]

While Reinhold Niebuhr recognized the need for "vocational pacifism," he was quick to point out the two distinctive philosophies of nonresistance and nonviolence, which supported the pacifist position in the United States. He charged that the first was a perfectionistic ethic seeking to maintain purity of life and morals; he charged that the latter sought to change the world into a community by means of a pragmatic pacifism. Neither could be accepted by the entire church, but both could be acknowledged as playing vital roles in the life of the church. There is a tension in an ethic which combines both love and justice, and this tension expresses itself in the life of the church through the appearance of minority voices.

Many Brethren feel themselves to be vocational pacifists, as is indicated by their primary concerns that individual conscience be recognized and that each individual follow his own conscience above all else in deciding his position. The statement concerning the Christian and war coming from the World Council of Churches at Amsterdam in 1948 recognized the pacifist position as one possibility for the Christian conscience. Brethren were grateful to find pacifists in other denominations also supporting this position, but at the same time were less certain that the pacifists alone were right in discerning God's will in this matter. Many of us were willing to recognize the other positions as containing Christian truth also. We desire official ecumenical recognition, but few espouse nonresistance and nonviolence with evangelistic vigor.

The *Brethren Service News* for October 1960 contained a typical comment about the Brethren reaction to public demonstration on disarmament. "The Brethren were conspicuous by their absence. We are still reluctant to engage in political action." In other words, *some* are sure that the pacifist witness needs to be made, but most are not sure that every Christian needs to make it.

The statement of the Church of the Brethren on war adopted at Annual Conference in 1957 reflects an attitude of vocational pacifism toward our own church membership as well as our place in the larger church.

"It is recognized ... that not all members will hold the beliefs which the church recommends. Some will feel conscientiously obligated to render full military service and others noncombatant military service. Some, on the other hand, may feel compelled to refuse even to register under a conscriptive law. Since the church desires to maintain fellowship with all who sincerely follow the guidance of conscience, it will respect such decisions, in spite of its disappointment that its message has not been taught better or comprehended more fully."[17]

We imply that a person who perceives that

the will of God for him is to be a non-pacifist is to be accepted in the church because he has sincerely followed his conscience. By so doing we make the definition of the church ambiguous. Is the church to be made up only of pacifists? Are those who follow their consciences in being non-pacifists following something else than the source from which the church makes its recommendations? What is the relationship of the Holy Spirit, the Scriptures, and our own denominational tradition?

Our ambiguity at this juncture of history indicates our willingness to recognize both pacifists and non-pacifists in the fellowship of the Body of Christ. We are willing to accept the assumption that God's will in this matter of war and peace differs for different individuals; some are called to make a clear and unmistakable pacifist witness along the lines of either nonresistance or nonviolence and others are called to serve in a military capacity in the fight against evil.

The assumptions of the vocational pacifists seem to be:

1. An uncompromising witness which shows the sinfulness of war is needed in the church of Christ and in the world.

2. Although God does not call all to make this testimony, he does call a significant minority and they are responsible to be obedient to the call.

3. Although God's will leads different individuals along different paths in the structuring of law and order, his will is always that truth be allowed to be heard from all persons.

4. The vocational pacifist is concerned that each Christian consciously seek and obey the will of God; moreover, he is concerned that each hear the claims of the pacifist position and obey if God so calls him.

ENDNOTES

1. October 27, 1950. "If you are faced with aggression, meet it, but team up with its social and economic means of solution."

2. John Horsch, *The Principle of Nonresistance as Held by the Mennonite Church*, second edition, revised (Scottdale, Pennsylvania: Mennonite Publishing House, 1940), pages 22-23. Quoted from E. Goetzinger, Vadians Deutsche Historische Schriften, Bd. 3, St. Gallen, 1877, page 501.

3. Harold S. Bender, *Menno Simons' Life and Writings* (Scottdale, Pennsylvania: Mennonite Publishing House, 1944), page 90.

4. Umphrey Lee, *The Historic Church and Modern Pacifism* (New York and Nashville: Abingdon-Cokesbury Press, 1943), page 150.

5. Rufus D. Bowman, *The Church of the Brethren and War* (Elgin: Brethren Publishing House, 1944), pages 43-44. Quoted from *Minutes of Annual Meetings, 1778-1909*, pages 9-10

6. *Ibid.*, page 44.

7. *Ibid.*, page 236.

8. *Ibid,* page 237.

9. *Ibid,* page 241.

10. *Ibid,* page 242.

11. According to W. Harold Row in an interview on April 17, 1960.

12. Reinhold Niebuhr, "Why I Leave the F.O.R.," in the *Christian Century* for January 3, 1934, pages 17-19.

13. Paul Tillich, "Beyond Religious Socialism," in the *Christian Century* for June 15 1949, pages 732-733.

14. His book, *Stride Toward Freedom* (New York: Harper and Brothers, 1958), should be read by every Christian, and especially by the Brethren.

15. See his *An Interpretation of Christian Ethics* (New York: Harper and Brothers, 1935).

16. *Ibid.,* pages 187-188.

17. Statement of the Church of the Brethren on War, adopted at Annual Conference. Richmond, Virginia. 1957 (Elgin: Brethren Press, 1957), page 4.

The Nuclear Dilemma,
With a Nod to Kierkegaard

If one will examine closely the account of the Exodus, he will discover that a strong east wind drove the waters back and allowed the Israelites to cross in safety before the Egyptian troops, ordered out to bring back the fleeing slaves, drowned in their attempt to follow. Their escape, seen in this perspective, was a coincidence of history. But to those who saw the governance of God, the awesomeness and unbelievable nature of what was taking place could not be thus described; rather, the Holy One was bringing about that event the consequences of which could not be understood at the time and the logic of which could never have been deduced from preceding events. Such is the dimension of the miraculous divine activity.

When Hosea's wife could not be faithful to him, the sociologists of the day said that it could be understood in the light of her background as a "priestess" at the high places. But to one who saw the divine governance, the former occupation of Gomer had passed judgment upon itself, and the God of Israel as breaking through to reveal his love and suffering over his unfaithful covenant people.

To any modern psychiatrist, whose ultimate
concern is the new knowledge he has
recently discovered, religion is "pleasing
father." And no one better illustrates the
validity of his proposition than Soren
Kierkegaard. But to any who believe in the
governance of God, Soren Kierkegaard has
etched into history the importance of the
individual's faith, the ultimate significance of
decision, and the precedence of the vertical
dimension of duty.

The Christian faith proclaims that God is ever
present and active in the life of the Church,
the history of mankind, and the created
order. Consciously or unconsciously, every
Christian affirms his belief in the divine
governance when he asks, "What is the will
of God for my life and the issues of my
epoch?"

Most of us are not creative geniuses; we ride
on the coattails of those who have
spearheaded the way. The cutting-edge
belongs to the few. Often we do not even see
the issues involved and would be only too
happy if our grandchildren were rightly taught
in historical perspective the important issues
decided by their forefathers.

Yet whenever we are placed in a situation that calls for decision we are obligated as Christians to respond "for the glory of God and our neighbor's good." When the issue is most crucial, we are the more earnestly commanded to seek the will of God in the spirit of Christ. The events of recent years demand of us that we reconsider an historical perplexity to the Christian Church in the new dimension of the Atomic Age. Some answers are possible now which have been impossible until the present time.

It is the popular assumption of our generation that the existing balance of power between the USA and the USSR preserves peace and prevents war. CORVAIR advertised on the back cover of *Time* magazine for July 20, 1959, that the Strategic Air Command was the "Underwriter of American Security" and its beneficiaries were "Free People Everywhere." We have learned that "airpower is peace power" and that the airmen of SAC have established that "peace is their profession." Many Christians believe that only as we are militarily powerful shall we be entitled to hold off tyranny and save the freedom of peaceful change.

But at the same time throughout the Church

49

of Jesus Christ there are those who are saying, "The prospect of a future war to be waged with the use of modern means of annihilation has created a new situation, in the face of which the Church cannot remain neutral. ... Atomic war is incapable of being used for the resolution of political conflicts because it destroys every presupposition of political resolution." 1 Indeed, only a week before the *Time* magazine appeared on the newsstands one Christian theologian, L. Harold DeWolf, who in the past has taken a traditional attitude toward war, was saying, "The story of blind Samson's suicidal revenge presents a shockingly close parallel to the present defense strategy of the United States. . . . The beginning of a return to sanity can come only when we face the plain fact that nothing can be defended by nuclear bombs, for annihilation is not defense. It is only insane, unchristian, suicidal vengeance . . . If martyrdom must be endured, we can choose the forgiving, reconciling love of Christ on the cross. rather than the mad revenge of blind Samson." 2

Christians are once again called by God to witness to his power and never-ending activity in the history of his children. The context of the decisions called for is illuminated by Soren Kierkegaard's *Fear and*

50

Trembling. His arguments concerning the nature of faith, exemplified in the story of Abraham and Isaac, seem to make the issues raised in the "nuclear dilemma" ring in the reader's ears with more clarity and urgency. The main body of the essay which follows is in its format a serious parody of Soren Kierkegaard's outline for *Fear and Trembling.*

I.   PRELUDE

God said, "Take your son, your only son Isaac, whom you love, and go to the land of Moriah, and offer him there as a burnt offering upon one of the mountains of which I shall tell you."

And Abraham lifted up his eyes and looked, and behold, behind him was a ram, caught in a thicket by his horns; and Abraham went and took the ram, and offered it up as a burnt offering instead of his son. (from Genesis 22).

The interpretation of Genesis 22 has undergone a radical change in the past century. The historic-cultural method of interpreting the Bible and the accumulating evidence of archeology have brought about significant differences in our understanding of the Scriptures. Our understanding of

God's "testing" of Abraham is significantly different from the way in which Soren Kierkegard understood the story. S. K. took the story at its face value; but for us the exposition by Walter Russell Bowie in the *Interpreter's Bible* forms the basis for any further interpretation.

"Here in the story of Abraham and Isaac there is imbedded the fact that once men not only practiced human sacrifice, but did it at what they thought was divine command. Suppose they did that now? Any man who thought of it, if his thoughts were detected, would be put in a mental hospital. Any man who actually carried it out would be convicted of murder and executed. . . . Why did this story of what was planned to be a human sacrifice get into the Bible? Because it was desired to show that Abraham's devotion to the God he worshiped was capable of going to the farthest point religion could reach. Human sacrifice was an actual custom among some of the Canaanite tribes. It was practiced for centuries. In the time of Elisha, ca. 800 B.C., in a crisis of battles for his capital, the king of Moab "took his eldest son ... and offered him for a burnt offering upon the wall" (II Kings 3: 27). 3 If men worshiping pagan deities could carry their religion to that terrific cost, how could Abraham show that his religion meant as much to him? Only by being willing to go as far as they did. So, in representing what went on in the mind of Abraham, the story has a deep and dramatic authenticity. Here was a great soul living in a crude age. He saw people around him offering up their children to show their faith and their obedience to false gods. In spite of the torment to his human love he could not help hearing an inward voice asking him why he should not do as much; and because that thought seemed to press upon his conscience he thought it was the voice of God. The climax of the story is the revelation that what the voice of God would ultimately say was something completely different from what Abraham in his first agony of acceptance had supposed. The climax is not the sacrifice of Isaac but the word from God that Isaac shall not be sacrificed. 4

II. A PANEGYRIC UPON ABRAHAM

Surely Abraham must have thought for a long time about what was involved before he actually set out for Mount Moriah. If the Canaanites could sacrifice their first-born to their gods, could Abraham do less for his? Perhaps even Abraham's forefathers, in their polytheistic worship, had sacrificed their eldest children. But the question was now Abraham's.

A familiar hymn reads, "God works in a mysterious way his wonders to perform ...." In the intense struggle within Abraham, God was at work. The conflict of loyalty to God and love of his son produced suffering. But in suffering, when all our powers of mind and body are concentrated at one point, especially in the crisis of life and death decisions, God can make himself known to us. And so to Abraham, in the midst of struggle, He spoke.

On the one hand was the obligation Abraham felt to render to God the same degree of devotion evidenced by others around him. On the other hand was his love for Isaac, his only son, born to him in his old age. At the culmination of the struggle on Mount Moriah, the still small voice of God was speaking to him.

Abraham had gone up on Mount Moriah a believer in human sacrifice; he came down no longer believing that God required human sacrifice of men. His understanding of the value of human life had changed. Surely God was with Abraham on Mount Moriah!

Our human experience too requires us to make decisions. How fortunate we would be and how great would be the measure of faith given by God's grace if we could say after the struggles on our "Mount Moriahs," Surely God was with us! Becoming a Christian involves looking to the example of Abraham in hopes that we too can discern the voice of God.

III. PROBLEMATA: PRELIMINARY EXPECTORATION

Kierkegaard sought to exalt faith, not to dismiss man's ability to think. He thought that faith went beyond or transcended what the thinking of man could prove or demonstrate, but this does not mean that he thought faith was in opposition to man's thought. It was not "believing what isn't true!"

"So the believing Christian not only possesses but uses his understanding, respects the universal human, does not put it down to lack of understanding if somebody is not a Christian; but in relation to Christianity he believes against the understanding and in this case also uses understanding . . . to make sure that he believes against the understanding. Nonsense therefore he cannot believe against the understanding, for precisely the understanding will discern that it is nonsense and will prevent him from believing it; but he makes so much use of the understanding that he becomes aware of the incomprehensible, and then he holds to this, believing against the understanding."5

The last sentence-paragraph of SK's "preliminary expectoration" also seems to follow this trend of thought: "It is now my intention to draw out from the story of Abraham the dialectical consequences inherent in it, expressing them in the form of problemata, in order to see what a tremendous paradox faith is, a paradox which is capable of transforming a murder into a holy act well-pleasing to God, a paradox which gives Isaac back to Abraham, which no thought can master, *because faith begins precisely there where thinking leaves off.*" 6

On the other hand, Kierkegaard was very disparing of Heglian philosophy, the dominant "system" of his day. He considered it an obstacle to the Christian faith. It may well be that some of his most cutting remarks against "reason" were directed at what he considered to be Hegel's abstract, unrelated-to-reality philosophy. One sentence in the early pages of *Fear and Trembling* reveals here, as elsewhere, his controversy with philosophy (naturally that which he knew in his own day): "Philosophy cannot and should not give faith, but it should understand itself and know what it has to offer and take nothing away, and least of all should fool people out of something as if it were nothing." 7

In this same vein of thought, Walter Lowrie comments on the *postscript* by writing, "'The infinitely interested subjective thinker' is contrasted by Climacus with the speculative philosopher who, as he is proud to claim, disinterestedly seeks to ascertain objective truth without any concern about his relation to it."8 He later states: "The leap is indeed a decisive *choice}* and as such it is an expression of the will. But this does not imply an antithesis between the intellect and the will, for the whole man, intellect, feeling and will, is involved in the choice." 9

The above quotations may modify or mitigate Kierkegaard's position too much; that is quite possible. It is in this spirit, however, that the rest of this paper will be understood.

To attempt to relate the "nuclear dilemma" to SK's paradox of faith may seem slightly ridiculous, but to some I feel sure that the decision to reject nuclear warfare will appear quite irrational. To the extent that this is true, I feel justified in discussing the choice involved within the context of Kierkegaard's paradox of faith. It will be obvious to the reader, however, that a modern interpretation of SK's exegesis of the story of Abraham and Isaac also modifies and puts into different perspective the "paradox of faith."

In the material that follows, each of the three problems as phrased by Kierkegaard is discussed in three different sections. First, there is a summary of what Kierkegaard himself has said. Secondly, there is an attempt to interpret the problem according to the contemporary exegesis of the story of Abraham and Isaac. Third, there is the attempt to illuminate the choice necessary in the "nuclear dilemma" in a modified framework of Kierkegaard's "paradox of faith."

IV. Problem I: "Is There a Teleological Suspension of the Ethical?"

Kierkegaard answers in the affirmative to each of the three problem-questions that he poses. To understand his answers, some definition of terms is in order.

"The ethical as such is the universal, and as the universal it applies to everyone, which may be expressed from another point of view by saying that it applies every instant." [10]

"As soon as the individual would assert himself in his particularity over against the universal he sins, and only by recognizing this can he again reconcile himself with the universal." [11]

But this mode of thought does not account for faith as SK has understood it to exist in Abraham. The universal is; "you shall love your son," yet Abraham is commanded to kill his son. Is he thus a murderer? Has he not fallen into sin by asserting his particularity over against the universal? No, for:

> "Faith is precisely this paradox, that the individual as the particular is higher than the universal, is justified over against it, is not subordinate but superior-yet in such a way, be it observed, that it is the particular individual who, after he has been subordinated as the particular to the universal, now through the universal becomes the individual who as the particular is superior to the universal, for the

fact that the individual as the particular stands in an absolute relation to the absolute."12

Abraham is absolutely responsible to God. This is his first obedience. The individual takes priority over the universal. This can only mean for SK that "the story of Abraham contains therefore a teleological suspension of the ethical." 13 And Kierkegaard is anxious to point out to the reader that Abraham was not simply another hero in Greek tragedy.

"The tragic hero still remains within the ethical. He lets one expression of the ethical find its *telos* in a higher expression of the ethical. ... With Abraham the situation was different. By his act he overstepped the ethical entirely and possessed a higher *telos* outside of it, in relation to which he suspended the former. For I should very much like to know how one would bring Abraham's act into relation with the universal, and whether it is possible to discover any connection whatever between what Abraham did and the universal . . . except the fact that he transgressed it. It was not for the sake of saving a people, not to maintain the idea of the state, that Abraham did this, and not in order to reconcile angry deities." 14

In Canaan it was the "universal" practice to sacrifice one's eldest son as the highest testimony of one's devotion to his god. The author of 2 Kings gives witness to the widespread custom. "He even burned his son as an offering, according to the abominable practices of *the nations whom the Lord drove out* before the people of Israel" (II Kings 16: 3).

Was not Abraham the chief patriarch of the Hebrews? Did not he, more than anyone else, have a duty to sacrifice his son to show that his tribe's devotion to their God was equal to the devotion of other tribes?

For Abraham not to sacrifice Isaac, to believe that God speaks differently to him, is to sin against the universal. And to his contemporaries it must have appeared that he had violated the judgment of the race, had gone against the universally accepted rite of religious devotion, and had subjected himself, his tribe, and his God to ridicule and shame.

Yet in our contemporary understanding, this is the only way we can meaningfully describe the paradox of faith for Abraham. More precisely, in his absolute relation to God, Abraham is called to stand over against the universal. That which other men have seen to constitute their highest duty, he finds to violate what God has now disclosed to him. Can the transition be logically deduced? Can the new be understood in light of the past?

Perhaps we need here to speak of "emergence" rather than "paradox," but regardless of semantics, the individual's relation to God remains the primary consideration. Perhaps we need to say that the universal has been transcended rather than suspended, but in either case, Abraham's action reflects his faith in God, and the rationalism of his contemporaries is shown to be void.

Consider the position taken by L. Harold DeWolf. He declares that engagement in or preparation for nuclear war is sin. To say this is to stand against the recognized universal ethic. Has he not "suspended" the universal, the ethical? Or has he fallen into sin by asserting his particularity over against the universal?

Chiseled into the foundation of the Christian-democratic heritage is Patrick Henry's famed declaration in St. John's Church of Richmond, "Give me liberty or give me death!"15 And in symbolic poetry the "Battle Hymn of the Republic" declares, "As He died to make men holy, let us die to make men free .... " To die in the defense of one's loved ones, to respond to the call of duty to country, to be willing to sacrifice for good when evil makes that necessary-this is the universal.

But when Dr. DeWolf renounces nuclear war and the "Underwriters of American Security" (the USAF Strategic Air Command), he renounces the "unequalled instrument of our national policy to maintain world peace" (from the back cover of *Time*). Does not this seem in direct opposition to the cherished values and accepted norms of Christian citizenship?

Dr. DeWolf would accept tyranny before he would drop the Bomb on Moscow. He would trust God's activity in the historical process before he would defend freedom in the traditional pattern of his forefathers. He would regard the words of Patrick Henry *now* to mean sin rather than virtue and courage.

Perhaps this is the meaning of the suspension of the ethical: that each generation must make its response to God and not to the universal. Perhaps this is the paradox: that faith appears utterly ridiculous to the unfaithful. 16

V. PROBLEM II: "IS THERE AN ABSOLUTE DUTY TOWARD GOD?"

For Kierkegaard, if the ethical is universal (binding on all at every instant), and that divine, then every duty would be a duty toward God. But in this usage of terms, "God" signifies the universal ethic and as such is only a tautology. On the other hand:

> "The paradox of faith is this, that the individual is higher than the universal, that the individual ... determines his relation to the universal by his relation to the absolute, not his relation to the absolute by his relation to the universal. The paradox can also be expressed by saying that there is an absolute duty toward God; for in this relationship of duty the individual as an individual stands related absolutely to the absolute. So when

in this connection it is said that it is a duty to love God, something different is said from that in the foregoing; for if this duty is absolute, the ethical is reduced to a position of relativity. From this, however, it does not follow that the ethical is to be abolished, but it acquires an entirely different expression, the paradoxical expression-that, for example, love to God may cause the knight of faith to give his love to his neighbor the opposite expression to that which, ethically speaking, is required by duty." 17

For SK, the story of Abraham and Isaac illustrates this. Ethically expressed, the father should love the son. But the "absolute relation" to God makes the ethical expression relative to the absolute duty of God's command-"sacrifice your son." The absolute duty takes precedence over the universal ethic.

In terms of the universal, Abraham would be a murderer, but in terms of the paradox his act is a *sacrifice--because* Abraham does not cease to love, although paradoxically his love of God and his love of Isaac are in opposition.

How different is a modern exegesis of Genesis 22! The tension - the conflicting pulls-the "paradox" - are all still present. But the duties are reversed! The universally recognized ethic requires that Abraham kill his son as a sacrificial offering. The command of God calls to Abraham to transcend the universal -- to emerge to a new understanding -- to stand forth in opposition to the universal. It is an absolute duty, a duty to God alone; the universally recognized demands are rejected.

The journey to Mount Moriah is one of conflict and struggle. The words to Isaac (that God will provide the sacrifice) are ambiguous, uncertain in their depth, and full of anxious reflection and meditation. Undoubtedly, as SK notes, most of the trip was in silence. On Mount Moriah the knife is raised-but never lowered. A ram appears in the thicket-the governance of God-and Abraham, *in faith,* offers it as the sacrifice instead of his son.

Abraham understands God in a new light. This relationship takes precedence over the unanimous consent of men that human sacrifice is demanded of the gods. (We shall cite the Aztecs and others if we need to prove our point about the "universal ethic!") Abraham can only respond that this is *his* duty to God, for he does not yet know how history or God shall judge his action. He responded in faith-and if you please, "over 70,000 fathoms!"

> Footnote: Have not the presuppositions of this section changed from the presuppositions of the first section in the discussion of this second problem? In light of the modern understanding of the story of Abraham, can we say and mean what SK meant when he said that there is a teleological suspension of the ethical? Has not his thesis, at least as it applies to Abraham, been shown now to be in error? Was not the universal *superseded* rather than *suspended?*

It would seem that Dr. DeWolf speaks "in faith" - "against the universal" - "of an absolute duty" when he says that engagement in or preparation for nuclear war is sin. The crucial point is not that this is a "vocation pacifism," but that by intention he makes his choice binding on every Christian. And his position has the characteristics of an absolute relation to God, superseding the recognized universal rationale.

The universal declares that any political ethic must be relevant to the situation and responsible to mankind in its implications. One must work within the compromises and the ambiguities of the political structure. Is the situation now reversed? Does our absolute duty to God require that we "draw a line" beyond which we separate ourselves from God?

Dr. DeWolf says that now in the name of justice, love of neighbor and law and order, that we are called upon to cease our involvement as Christians in the preparation for nuclear war. Are we called upon to lay down the very weapons by which our security has been guaranteed (according to some) and by which we have defended the free world? Is justice and civilization according to law now upheld by some other means?

If I understand Dr. DeWolf correctly, he is saying that we cannot be loyal to God as revealed in Jesus Christ and at the same time threaten any of the children of God with "massive retaliation"- regardless of the circumstances. "Love" and "massive retaliation" are not two prongs of a paradox, they are a contradiction--both to men and to God. Thus there is involved an absolute duty to God by temporal or "universal" considerations. The absolute duty requires our faith in God's activity in history in all men, but especially in the Church, and calls us to reject our faith in nuclear weapons as our ultimate source of strength.

Footnote: Although the contemporary existential situation of Dr. DeWolf may look as precarious as the contemporary existential situation of Abraham, I feel sure that Dr. DeWolf would not believe that there has been a teleological suspension of the ethical. I think he would say rather that "New occasions teach new duties; time makes ancient good uncouth" -that a new dimension in our understanding of God is emerging on the historic scene and that it supersedes the old.

VI. Problem III: "Was Abraham Ethically Defensible in Keeping Silent about His Purpose before Sarah, before Eleazar, before Issac?"

When we consider again that the ethical is the universal, and that the universal is manifest and revealed, it is evident that concealment involves either sin or a temptation in this frame of reference.

"If there is not a concealment which has its ground in the fact that the individual as the individual is higher than the universal, then Abraham's conduct is indefensible. ..." 18

Hegelian philosophy would demand that the individual come out of his particularity and identify himself with the universal. But if this is so, Abraham is indefensible.

Examples from Greek tragedy and modern drama are used by Kierkegaard to show that concealment is a common motif in these, but also to show that there is an absolute distinction between concealment in aesthetics and ethics, and concealment in the paradox of faith. In Greek tragedy, fate conceals its workings from the tragic heroes, revealing its purposes in the universal ethic which through suffering the tragic hero comes to recognize. In modern drama which has given up the notion of fate, "When the hero ensnared in the aesthetic illusion thinks by his silence to save another man, then it (aesthetics) requires silence and rewards it. On the other hand, when the hero by his action intervenes disturbingly in another man's life, then it requires revelation."[19]

But in both Greek and modern drama, concealment takes place in light of the universal ethic. However, Abraham stands in an absolute relation to the absolute; his action is not that of a tragic hero in an aesthetic role.

> "Aesthetics permitted, yea, required of the individual silence, when he knew that by keeping silent he could save another. This is already sufficient proof that Abraham does not lie within the circumference of aesthetics. His silence has by no means the intention of saving Isaac, and in general his whole task of sacrificing Isaac for his own sake and for God's sake is an offense to aesthetics, for aesthetics can well understand that I sacrifice myself, but not that I sacrifice another for my own sake."[20]

Abraham's action is defensible only in the paradox of faith. He stands in an absolute relation to God, and this particularity is higher than the universal. He has made the infinite movement of resignation by renouncing his claim to Isaac. "We see then that after making this movement he made every instant the next movement, the movement of faith by virtue of the absurd,"[21] thus being willing to sacrifice Isaac because of God's demand. Abraham's silence was defensible because only he and he alone could act in obedience to God's demand upon him and no other.

If the crucial issue was human sacrifice, then it is doubtful that Abraham was silent in the way which SK ascribes to him. Perhaps he was silent most of the time--in deep agony over the situation. And perhaps Sarah did share his agony. Perhaps he was relatively silent until he reached Mount Moriah because he himself did not know what the final outcome would be; and his words of "irony" contained no real answer to Isaac's question because he himself did not know what the answer would be. The command of the Canaanite gods was evident: no one could expect prosperity, posterity, and protection (as well as recognition by his neighbors) in this land of milk and honey who did not show his supreme devotion to the gods.

The real solitude of Abraham came *after* his descent from Mount Moriah; it was the anxiety of trying to communicate to his family, his tribe, and his neighbors the truth and validity of the course of action which he *did* pursue on Mount Moriah. For on one side, his action has the appearance of extreme egoism, and on the other side his action is in obedience to God's will." "The demoniacal has the same characteristic as the divine inasmuch as the individual can enter into an absolute relation to it."23

The Canaanites (as well as the Hebrews) could well argue that Abraham's action was out of selfishness and not out of obedience to God. One needs only examine the Biblical record to realize how long the proponents of human sacrifice continued to state their case! Demonic or prophetic? It was that question which "silenced" for many years Abraham's ability to communicate.

Christians cannot engage in or prepare for nuclear warfare. Does this arise as the result of selfishness in the face of possible destruction, a sort of last minute grasping for security, or does it arise out of the love of God for his children in which he sheds the light of a new perspective on the context of international events and world history?

The silence (if we may use SK's terminology with different meaning) of Dr. DeWolf is similar to the silence of Abraham after Mount

Moriah according to our contemporary understanding: it is the solitude of a position spelled out as a result of obedience to Deity and not obedience to the recognized norm; it is a solitude arising out of the desire to communicate, which desire is thwarted because the action has the ambiguity of being either demoniacal or obedience to the Absolute; it is the solitude of the prophet, the silence of the misunderstood.

The silence is broken only by the Spirit which witnesses within, "Resolve no more to cancel your testimony to Christ by trust in the vengeful bomb."[24]

VII. Epilogue: "Is There a Teleological Suspension of the Ethical?"

The logic of SK's interpretation of Abraham's action leads to an affirmative conclusion.

A contemporary interpretation of Abraham's action destroys the historical foundation of SK's interpretation.

The existential basis of SK's answer no longer exists; we cannot think of other examples to take its place.

An examination of Abraham's action rightly understood and an examination of a contemporary ethical-faith decision leads to a different conclusion in regard to SK's original question.

While the universally recognized ethic is *superseded* as a result of God's continuing activity in human history, it is never *suspended.*

There is a leap of faith and a primary duty toward God in crucial choices; these are most evident when the struggle for decision is most intense.

In the nuclear dilemma has appeared the *kairos* for our epoch; there is only faith or unfaith in response.

ENDNOTES

1. *Documents of the Contemporary German Church Struggle,* edited by John H. Yoder (New York: Church Peace Mission, 1959), p. 11.

2. "Blind Samson or Christ." Lecture given by Dr. L. Harold DeWolf at Garrett Biblical Institute, July 8, 1959, *passim.*

3. Dr. Bowie could also have cited Manasseh's sacrifice of his son (II Kings 21: 6), the same deed by Ahaz (II Kings 16: 3), and the sacrifice of Hiel of Bethel, who laid the foundation of Jericho "at the cost of his first-born" according to the prophecy of Joshua (I Kings 16: 34 and Joshua 6: 26).

4. George A. Buttrick (ed.), *The Interpreter's Bible* (New York-Nashville: Abingdon-Cokesbury Press, 1952), Volume I, pp. 642-646.

5. Soren Kierkegaard, *Concluding Unscientific Postscript,* trans. by David F. Swenson (Princeton: Princeton University Press, 1941), p. 504.

6. Soren Kierkegaard, *Fear and Trembling,* trans. by Walter Lowrie (Garden City, New York: Doubleday & Co., 1954), p. 64. (Underlining mine.)

7. *Ibid.,* p. 44.

8. Walter Lowrie, *A Short Life* of *Kierkegaard* (Princeton: Princeton University Press, 1942), p. 171.

9. *Ibid.,* p. 174.

10. Soren Kierkegaard, *Fear and Trembling,* p. 64.

11. *Ibid.,* p. 65.

12. *Ibid.,* p. 66.

13. *Ibid.,* p. 77.

14. *Ibid.,* p. 69 f.

15. Richmond, Virginia, March 23, 1775, at the

second Virginia convention.

16. "Whom the gods would destroy they first make mad with power." (One of four lessons of history attributed to Charles Beard, American historian.)

17. Soren Kierkegaard, *Fear and Trembling*, p. 80.

18. *Ibid.*, p. 91.

19. *Ibid.*, p. 96.

20. *Ibid.*, p. 121 f.

21. *Ibid.*, p. 128.

22. *Ibid.*, p. 81.

23. *Ibid.*, p. 106.

24. L. Harold DeWolf, Lecture cited, p. 5.

The Pax Atomica

Decisions that lead to both justice and security in the reconciliation of nations are the desired goal of Christian concern. The fact that such decisions within the specific context of the nuclear dilemma are not always clear and distinct reflects a general Biblical teaching that mankind lives outside the Garden of Eden and the specific problem that people strive for political ends even within the framework of the balance of terror.

Some Christians argue for unilateral nuclear disarmament. They seek the means whereby nations and people may solve their international conflicts without resort to unlimited warfare. Is this a utopian goal? There are other Christians who answer in the affirmative on the basis of their proof-text; "And you will hear of wars and rumors of wars; see that you are not alarmed; for this must take place, but the end is not yet" (Matthew 24:6).

If one takes into account moral achievements of the past and the impact of technological advances, it becomes conceivable that the major aim of the nuclear pacifists - the abolishing of global total wars - is a legitimate and possible goal for finite men. Four decades of a *pax atomica* in a world of intense rivalry, worldwide peace movements, and the growth of international organizations would be lines of evidence to suggest the probability of another major change in human relations. Are there reasons for believing that the abolition of world wars can take place in human history?

History is not without its moral achievements. Significant changes in the interrelationships of men and groups have taken place. The changes do not mean that evil has been overcome, but they do mean that certain social practices have been attacked as evil structures and have been changed. The practices have been superseded by other structures in which the divine and the demonic continue to vie for supremacy. Nevertheless, issues at stake in the previous structure are resolved. There are important precedents in biblical history and in church history to support the contention that specific moral objectives are approximated within history. There are "achievements" which represent the victory of good over evil, even though these achievements are tempered by the realization that the final triumph of love for the Christian remains beyond history.

The Old Testament gives evidence that human sacrifice was the practice of numerous peoples in Canaan before and during Hebrew history.[1] That it was practiced at times by the Hebrews themselves, convinced the Deuteronomic historians of the apostasy of certain periods of Israelite history.[2] God's revelation to Abraham, and Abraham's consequent turning from the sacrifice of Isaac, marked the beginning of conscience among the Hebrew people on this religious practice. God's command not to sacrifice Isaac raised man's vision beyond this barbaric practice. The battle in this instance raged for centuries. Indeed, the Judean king, Manasseh, was guilty of sacrificing his firstborn 150 years before the Exile, and many centuries after the time of Abraham!

The significant point here is not that "human nature" was changed, but that a religious-moral institution embedded in society was challenged by the revelation of God to Abraham, and in time recognized for what it was - - contrary to the will of God. The attitude of men toward that institution changed, and human sacrifice itself was abolished as an acceptable religious practice. Herein we have a clear example of a specific break with the past in which one level of moral and religious obligation was superseded by another level (animal sacrifice) more in accord with the will of God.

An analogy can be found in the present crisis. John Hick writes in regard to the nuclear dilemma: "War becomes inevitable only within the context of the distinctive manner of life adopted by mankind through the ages. But that whole manner of life is itself largely 'contrary to the Mind of Christ,' and modern warfare, as an incident within it, constitutes a supreme expression of man's corporate disobedience to the divine will."[3] If one substitutes "human sacrifice" for "modern war" in the above quotation, it is evident that the same reasoning may be applied to the patriarchal period. Human sacrifice was then, as modern warfare is now, a "supreme expression of man's corporate disobedience to the divine will."

A Christian interpretation of history must allow for the fact that human sacrifice was challenged and rooted out of history during the ancient period; so now our understanding of history must be such as will at least allow for the deep transformation of the problem of war as it reaches a crucial state in the modern atomic age. This does not mean that mankind will not continue to live "contrary to the Mind of Christ," but it does proclaim that God is always active in history and that his people are given the power to challenge the diabolical outrages of this world.

Technological developments bring about changes in social institutions also. New factors in history call for new responses. While the goals of governments - - justice and security - - do not change, the means whereby they are achieved may change as the result of cultural transformation. The possible abolition of global war is no exception. The type of change that may be envisaged is described sociologically as follows: "The truth is that war is a multi-purpose and even an all-purpose procedure. The reason is clear; in a society that has not yet acquired its normal organs, the functions of the community can be fulfilled only by individuals, driven by their own interests and according to the law of functional substitution. Disorder, arising from the neglect of social needs is expressed, in conflicts between members of the social body. War is a way of solving these conflicts, a substitute method of procedure that allows one of the neglected social tasks to be performed by transfer of functions."[4] Developments in military science have now brought us to a stage of history where mankind must abolish war and acquire the normal organs of community regulation. The problem can no longer be neglected. We must outgrow our global wars or be abolished by them.

It is not unusual that technological changes figure in religious and moral problems in history; new discoveries and inventions effect the relations between people - - and it is these relationships that are the substance of ethical problems and decisions. One may cite the following as examples. Martin Luther's conviction that the Bible was pre-eminent in value for teaching the Christian faith, and his translation of the New Testament into the vernacular had significant repercussions because of the invention of the printing press (1425). Together, these events brought about changes and crises that included their impact on the Reformation itself. The technological factor was of course not the sole causative factor of the Reformation, but without the printing press an entirely different result might have been expected.[5]

As another example, chattel slavery lost its hold in the United States, not only because of the moral indignation against it, but also because the cotton gin made it economically less desirable than earlier. "Slavery has long since been repudiated in most of the world, not least because machines made it superfluous and because it is an offense against moral law. The same is true of war; war is in an atomic age incompatible with the principles of Christian ethics, not because the horrors it creates are quantitatively increased, but because qualitatively its character has been basically changed."[6]

We do not mean to argue at this point that

slavery and war may be compared as institutions on a one-to-one ratio as is done in the above quotation. War is the *result* of conflict; slavery was a *source* of conflict. War comes about from the use of force as an *ultima ratio;* chattel slavery was more directly the product of a warped structuring of the social order. Slavery was *abolished* through the *changing* of the law; war can be *transformed* through the *bringing into existence* of *international law.*

The new situation in history results from a change brought about by what man has discovered. The discovery itself does not bring about the change, but the difference it makes in the potentialities available to mankind changes the context of decision, and makes imperative new responses on the part of men. Thus, only as the imagination grasps the new situation can new decisions be made, and only as the atomic age becomes real to us can we solve its problems.[7] In other words, we are to find ways of combating evil, even with radically limited use of force, while at the same time avoiding the type of global warfare that has brought such terrible destruction to the world in our century. "Perhaps the new frontier for ethics in a space age is to cultivate the concept of the limited war for specific objectives and to seek elimination of total nuclear war fought for absolutistic ends."[8]

It must be concluded that to seek to prevent and to abolish total global wars is a justifiable and binding moral objective for the church in this epoch of history. Such an objective can represent a kairotic moment in the life of the church if there is a faithful response on the part of the community of the disciples of Christ. In light of the responsibilities of the Christian to love the neighbor, the judgment that total nuclear war is an evil in which the Christian cannot participate is certainly valid. In other words, the nuclear pacifist rejection of total nuclear warfare as a justifiable *ultima ratio* is to be seen as a realistic historical goal, and not only as a messianic hope.

To argue for the abolition of war in a world society in which one seeks to preserve the values of freedom and order, requires both a statement of what the abolition of war is *not*, and a statement of that which is sought in place of war. George Kennan admirably states that the abolition of war does not mean the abolition of force; "Force is, and always will be, an indispensable ingredient in human affairs; the alternative to a hopeless kind of force is never no-force-at-all. A first step away from the horrors of the atom must be an adequate development of agencies of force more flexible, more discriminate, and less suicidal in their effects."[9]

But to affirm that compulsory power is ever present in the affairs of men is not enough. Modifications in application and relevance are possible. It is imperative that man learn to control the power he now possesses so that he may strive to achieve high goals and purposes. To attain both freedom and order for a world society requires the development of an international ethos. Only such an ethos will provide the foundation for world organization, law, and cooperation. As Sylvester Theisen states: "Our first moral responsibility is to avoid war without losing our basic freedoms and without destroying the growth of world understanding."[10] In the same article, he later makes an elaboration on the above comment which points to the positive emphasis which we need if we are to achieve the two polar goals of freedom and order. "Our aim must be to develop an awareness of the brotherhood of all men, a living world community, an operative political organization based on the rule of law for the entire world. Emphasis on military strategy and weapons will not achieve that kind of world. Military means are necessary but not adequate means. They are proportionate to defense needs but not to the creative struggle which will carry us beyond the present impasse."[11]

The game theorists today have made a serious attempt to calculate the results of deterrence strategy among nations. But even in game theory the limitations on calculation are severe. "What worries me is the fact that the total situation with which the theorists deal also contains extremely broad parameters of so qualitative a nature that no one could attribute numerical values to them. Some of these parameters are among the most important. ... For example, they include such matters as the enemy's intentions, as well as his strength and capacity; the resolution of our people; the capacity of a country to restore itself economically when it has suffered a degree of devastation well beyond anything that lives within human comprehension — let alone experience - and other matters equally vague. These are vitally important issues. But they are not numerical issues, and probably never can be made such, even if they were ever to come within our experience."[12] Values and predictions about the future are inseparably mixed; yet it is in these areas of ambiguity that crucial decisions are needed.

That total global wars should be abolished is a realistic goal shared by many nuclear pacifists and nuclear realists, but not accomplished as easily as the formula of "unilateral nuclear disarmament" would suggest. Civilized societies have resorted to law to bring order out of chaos within nations in the past. To attain world order through the establishment of law is more in accord with man's past history.

It is commonly argued by the nuclear pacifists that just war theory means that no all-out nuclear war could possibly be just, and therefore it cannot be just to possess and threaten to use nuclear weapons. However, this line of reasoning depends upon its reverse statement, that is, that the mere existence of nuclear weapons implies that they will be used in an all-out nuclear war. It is this later and primary assumption or implication that must be denied as an *inevitable* relationship. The existence of the nuclear weapons makes possible many things — one of which might be their use in an all-out nuclear war if man so intends and wills. But it is also possible that the weapons could be retained by nations as a deterrent to aggression and defense measure until other forms of international control emerge.

Mankind has entered a new era - the atomic age. As this epoch of history has emerged, it becomes increasingly clear that man now stands *between* two possibilities of the use of military power. On the one hand, as in the past, and yet not in the past, there exists limited power within his control which he can direct and use toward rational ends of international law and peace with justice. On the other hand, unique to the atomic age in which he now lives, man has the potential to unleash unlimited power that can bring about widespread chaos and destruction beyond his ability to calculate and channel.

Before the atomic age, man "stood on top" of the military power available to him. Potential destructive power was limited and within control. Man now has available nuclear power that is unlimited in its capacity to destroy. A technological leap has been made that allows power in the atomic age to dwarf all power of previous historical epochs. Man now "stands between" the possibilities of the use of violent power. He is "above" that force that may be used to achieve rationally controlled ends; he is "below" that power which brings about mutually self-destructive results for those who engage in its use. To keep in view these two poles is to argue that there must be drawn "a sharp distinction between the nuclear weapons of total destruction (including the tactical atomic weapons) and the so-called conventional weapons."[13] It is necessary technologically and conceptually to distinguish between limited non-atomic military power and unlimited nuclear military power in the making of ethical judgments.

The possibility of limited non-atomic warfare still exists. There is violent power within the control of man that can be used in limited ways to maintain law and order, and to secure recognition of the demands and rights of involved groups and nations. The many limited wars since the Second World War and the use of United Nations' police forces in several troubled areas substantiate this assertion. That is not to say that all limited use of force is justified, but only to say that the atomic age means that a redoubling of efforts must be made to effect a discipline for the radical limitation of the conventional means of warfare now available to men and nations.

In this area of the limited use of force, we may expect to see develop many techniques for the employment of varied types of power to accomplish political, social, and economic ends. "Warfare" will involve conventional armaments, guerilla tactics, nonviolent resistance, underground warfare, economic blockades, and no doubt other forms of limited conflict. One result of the emergent atomic possibility has been to open the door to numerous non-atomic possibilities. Mao Tse-Tung's writings on guerrilla warfare and Mahatma Gandhi's techniques of nonviolence are illustrative of such develop-ments, even though in divergent forms. [14] Both Asian leaders have developed concepts that have revolutionized the techniques of "warfare." Although at opposite ends of the spectrum regarding the use of violence and nonviolence, the two are similar in their recognition of the needed support of the local populace, the need for education of both "troops" and people regarding objectives, and their insistence on highly-trained and disciplined units within the movement.

It is in regard to atomic military power that there exists an urgent need to recognize the radical nature of the unlimited power that is now possessed by man. If used in an uncontrolled way, this power would catastrophically change man's history on the planet. It will not do to eliminate or renounce these atomic weapons, nor can we ignore or deny their presence. Rather, we must develop that discipline which accepts and acknowledges our possession of unlimited destructive power, yet refuses to use it to bring about self-destruction. [15] We must find and follow those policies which make civilized life possible, despite the freedom to destroy or alter that civilized life. We may see in this area the continued development of new weapons systems. In and of itself this need not be alarming; if, however, international security comes to be seen as solely dependent upon a military balance of terror, then such a false trust and analysis must be regarded as wrong and dangerous. No nation dare rely solely upon military power for its political, social, and economic security; for to do so is to be blind to the multidimensional configuration of elements which constitute a nation's power to advance its aims and objectives.

Thus, we face the danger of an *implosion.* Unlimited indiscriminate destruction could result either from an escalation of limited war, or from the actual use of the available thermonuclear bombs. To prevent escalation, demands radically limiting the use of conventional weapons, and finding other means (such as non-violence or the use of an international police force) for negotiating and resolving conflict situations. To seek the freedom and order of a responsible society, and to do so out of love for neighbor and concern for justice, means that even in the atomic age people must make calculations which acknowledge the tension between the ideal and the concrete realities.

Nuclear power and nuclear weapons will continue to exist. As *George* Kennan points out, these weapons "are conditioned at bottom by political differences and rivalries. To attempt to remove the armaments before removing these substantive conflicts of interest is to put the cart before the horse."[16] It must be recognized that as long as the nations of the world lack an international framework of law and order within which their differences may be settled, they will need to rely on other sources available to them for protection and defense. A minimum stabilized deterrence is essential as a check against aggression and is justified as a means of self-defense. It must also be recognized, however, that an all-out nuclear war would mean mutual annihilation and moral failure.

The alternative to an unjust use of nuclear weapons is not the abandonment of them to others. Rather: "Nuclear weapons must be maintained by us now until we can achieve effective international arms control. Good works are not a substitute for armed power to resist aggressors. But neither is armed might a substitute for the imagination and talent, for the energy and money that must be applied to the non-military areas of international existence." [17]

Although the Cuban missile crisis in the fall of 1962 showed that two of the great powers were willing to go to the very edge of nuclear warfare when the interests of both were at stake, it should be observed that the existence of a balance of terror has for a number of years kept limited the "warfare" between great powers. [18] Probably mutual fear and mutual recognition of consequences have restrained all sides. Nevertheless, faced with the possibility of the use of self-destructive atomic military power, rulers must be urged by the church to affirm a paradoxical limitation in regard to atomic warfare. Possession but not use of the nuclear weapons is required.

The need to avoid the kind of all-out global war that has characterized the 20th century should not be minimized, however. Man's new capacity for war must be restrained. "A morally good man need not protest against nuclear weapons as such, but a moral man in this nuclear age is obliged to work zealously, courageously, and with imagination for the kind of world which will make war obsolete."[19]

The awakening of the Christian conscience to the evil of war is perhaps one of the most significant landmarks of the century in the history of the social teachings of the Christian church. The most important Christian ecumenical studies on international affairs have proclaimed war to be contrary to the will of God and destructive of man's civilizations. However, even in the midst of this, crucial decisions faced on the level of foreign policy and recommendations to national governments, to which Christians are loyal as citizens, find important divergencies in proposed programs.

On the one hand, some believe that the existence of absolute weapons has served to maintain a degree of stability and order in the world; on the other hand, peoples have lived in fear that intentionally or accidentally the megaton weapons might be used in a suicidal war. In other words, there is the continuing prevention of total war partially by the presence of the nuclear deterrent systems, but there is at the same time the risk that the deterrent systems will break down through accident or willful malice. Total war is now ruled out, but the threat of the use of force has served for four decades to restrain total warfare and maintain some degree of international stability.

While all-out nuclear war could never be an act of justice for the Christian, the use of the nuclear weapons as a deterrent is justified; for it makes a military contribution to the present *pax atomica.* (That which leads the nuclear pacifist to draw another conclusion is his understanding of nuclear weapons as inherently evil.) The role which nuclear weapons can and do play in international relations is to create a military deterrent against unlimited aggression and total war.

There are limitations on a strategy of deterrence, however. The limitations contribute to the instability of the pax atomica, and make the calculation of consequences with respect to the future very inexact. A strategy of deterrence assumes a stable balance of nuclear forces, but no such balance is ever permanent in the face of dynamic national powers and the inevitable changes of history. There is always the risk, even in the contemporary situation, that the balance win not remain stable. The present arms race can be very destabilizing and a grave threat to any detente relationship among the nuclear powers.

ENDNOTES

1. Cf. 2 Kings 3:27 (the King of Moab). 1 Kings 16:34 (Hie! of Bethel), and 2 Kings 16:3 (King Ahaz).

2. Cf. the reign of Manasseh and the sacrifice of his son (2 Kings 21:6).

3. John H. Hick, "The Structure of the War Problem," *Studies in Christian Social Commitment,* edited by John Ferguson (London: Independent Press, 1954), p, 25.

4. J. T. Delos, "The Sociology of Modern War and the Theory of Just War," *Cross Currents,* 8 (Summer 1958), p.263.

5. Lewis Mumford discusses the printing press in a slightly broader perspective in one of his essays, but the point in relation to the interpretation of history remains the same. "No single invention, probably, has had more radical effects upon the social order than printing from movable types; for at one stroke it broke the class monopoly of culture for the first time: he who learned to read progressively had access to every part of the social heritage in a society whose boundaries were in process of continued extension. That was, without

doubt, a gigantic social gain; for it laid the basis not merely for a democratic system of government but for a democratic culture; just as the machine generally, by raising the burden of servile human labor, had made it possible to achieve leisure and education without slavery." Lewis Mumford, *In the Name of Sanity* (New York: Harcourt, Brace and Company, 1954), p. 48.

6. Gerd Burkhardt, "War and Peace in a Technical Age," *The Student World,* 53 (1960), p. 433.

7. "Like the villagers on the side of Vesuvius returning and abiding over the centuries in the shadow of eventual destruction, most of us lead our lives with only spasmodic twinges of awareness and desperation." Louis Henkin, *Arms Control and Inspection in American Law* (New York: Columbia University Press, 1958), p. 1.

8. Edward Long, Jr., "Ethical Problems in a Space Age," *Religion in Life,* 30 (Summer 1961), p, 370.

9. George F. Kennan, *Russia, the Atom and the West* (New York: Harper and Brothers, 1957, 1958), pp, 56-57.

10. Sylvester P. Theisen, "Man and Nuclear Weapons," *American Benedictine Review,* 14 (September 13), p, 379.

11. *Ibid.*, p. 383.

12. Sir Solly Zuckerman, "Judgment and Control in Modern Warfare," *Foreign Affairs,* 40 (January 1962), p. 210.

13. Paul Tillich, "The Nuclear Dilemma - - A Discussion," *Christianity and Crisis* 21 (November 13, 11), p. 204.

14. See Mao Tse-Tung, *Guerrilla Warfare,* translated by

Samuel B. Griffith (New York: Frederick A. Praeger, 1961). First published in China in 1937. Also Homer A. Jack, ed, *The Gandhi Reader* (New York: Grove Press, Inc., 1956).

15. "There is an ambiguous element in sin which is self-destructive and yet self-preserving. Pragmatically one can rely on the rationality of sinful men not to destroy themselves, but morally this does nothing about the tension and destructive nature of sin as it finds expression in forms which are not totally destructive. Sin checks itself only at the point of annihilation, and to rest upon this without attempting to avoid sin's lesser consequences is to act immorally." James W. Ware, Jr., "Some Problems Involved in the Consideration of the Ethical Implications of Nuclear Warfare." An unpublished paper submitted in a course taught by Dr. Creighton Lacy at Duke University, June 2, 1961, pp. 24-25.

16. George Kennan, op. cit., p. 28.

17. Jacquard H. Rothchild, "Can Peace Be Guaranteed?" *Bulletin of Atomic Scientists,* 17 (November 1961), p. 387.

18. The border warfare between Russia and China should not be forgotten; it has been just as "explosive" as was the Cuban missile crisis.

19. Sylvester P. Theisen, op. cit., p. 384.

This article was first published in Brethren Life and Thought: "The Pax Atomica," 32 (Winter, 1987), 45-52. Used with Permission.

Paradox in the Nuclear Age

At times history seems to demand a clear break with the past—as in the case of human sacrifice and chattel slavery. At other times new meanings emerge within older structures to transform their significance--as in the case of woman's role in society and the family and the role of all citizens in government. In the present nuclear age both continuity and discontinuity seem to be demanded. If men are to stand against tyranny, continuity with the willingness to defend democratic social institutions is necessary; if men are to preserve their civilized life on earth, discontinuity with the willingness to participate in war with modern technology is imperative.

The Christian response to the nuclear dilemma has resulted in two forceful positions being expressed by just war theorists with the Church. Undoubtedly a tension--almost a contradiction-- has been created. This paradox of thought and action needs to be recognized and understood. If it is not urgent for world peace that the tension immediately be resolved, it is important and urgent for church activity in international affairs that the paradox be explicated so that representatives of both positions may discover areas of cooperation toward common ends. It would appear to be premature to resolve the paradox at this moment of history. It is as important now to understand the contrasting forces at work as it is to bring about a resolution of the paradox which would omit or slight vital and essential ethical concerns.

The basic position of the nuclear pacifists calls for unilateral renunciation of the megaton weapons. This position represents one ethic in response to the nuclear dilemma and represents a dimension of ethical concern for Christians to take seriously. The counter-position of the nuclear realists contends that we cannot abandon the possession of nuclear weapons. This realist position represents a new application of the classic "just war" ethic and this also is a dimension of Christian concern in the nuclear deadlock.

There would appear to be no one specific program of action which all Christians can be called to follow. The tension that exists between the nuclear pacifist and nuclear realist positions arises as a result of the dual demands which history makes on the contemporary great powers; these same dual demands account for the present seemingly contradictory positions taken by Christian ethicists who traditionally have espoused some form of the just war theory.

Recognition of the existence of a paradox of Christian ethical response regarding the use of nuclear weapons appeared early in England and Germany. The statements reflect the impact of the arguments of each position and recognize the merits and values of both. In that sense the Christian message cannot be said to be exhausted in either program, but at the same time the Christian message cannot be stated in one perspective apart from the other. It would seem to be such a perspective that the following statements represent.

The earliest indication of a paradox came from a study group of the British Council of Churches. The report was issued in 1946--soon after the atomic age had so dramatically burst into history. It was prophetic in that it recognized two logical and intuitive responses to the atomic crisis on the part of Christians.

"The possibility that an uncalculating refusal to have anything to do with methods of warfare involving wholesale massacre, and the acceptance of the political consequences arising out of such a refusal, is a duty demanded of us by the present historical crisis, and one which every serious mind must weigh. . . .

Over against the seemingly unconditional character of this demand has to be set the no less insistent Christian responsibility to defend the fundamental rights and liberties of men and the institutions through which in our society these are affirmed, protected and developed."[1]

The Commission went on to evaluate the two possibilities; no unanimous conclusion was reached although the majority accepted a position similar to nuclear realism. They pointed out as decisive that "no effective means has thus far been suggested of deterring a would-be aggressor except the fear of reprisals."[2]

But the study group did not draw the conclusion that one answer was acceptable to the Church and the other answer was unacceptable. Rather they said:

"We do not believe that the Church is able with its present insight to pronounce between the two alternatives. It must throw the shield of its protection and sympathy over those who make either choice. Each is the expression of loyalty to one side of Christian obligation. The one is a response to the claims of what presents itself as a moral absolute, and to an instinctive conviction that the future of the Church as the Body of Christ cannot be staked in a conflict in which there is no place left for mercy and the individual person counts for nothing at all. For those who make this choice the end of citizenship has come, since society has taken a course in which no Christian meaning has been found. The other decision is an attempt to discharge in the most desperate of situations the obligation which by God's appointment men owe to the temporal order; for those who make it the greatness of the crisis is a crowning reason why citizenship should be affirmed."3

The paradox of the arguments is clearly stated. The report understands that the Christian is torn between two alternatives in response to the nuclear dilemma. This affects the Church in both its preaching to people and its advice to governments.

A study group in Germany reached similar conclusions. The "Heidelberg theses" resulted from study and discussion at the University of Heidelberg.

These theses represent an attitude which can be taken toward the existing tension of the responses of nuclear pacifism and nuclear realism in the nuclear confrontation. Coming later than the British study, they state more clearly and in succinct form the essential nature of the paradox being described. The theses state demands binding on all Christians (1-4), estimates of the current dilemma (5-6), the two Christian responses (7-8), and advice which the Church can give to individuals and governments (9-11). They are:

(1) World peace has become the condition essential for life in the technological age.

(2) Christ demands from each of us a special role in the making of peace.

(3) War must be overcome in a lasting and progressing effort.

(4) Daily participation in this work for peace is our plain, simple and obvious duty.

(5) The way to world peace leads through a period of danger to justice and freedom if the classical justification of war is denied.

(6) We must seek to understand the disagreement of consciences affected differently by the dilemma of atomic weapons as complementary handles.

(7) The Church must acknowledge the renunciation of atomic weapons as a Christian way of acting.

(8) The Church must acknowledge the support of the attempt to secure a peace in freedom through the existence of atomic weapons as today also a possible Christian way of acting.

(9) For soldiers in an atomic-weapon equipped army this means: Those who must say "B" must reckon with what "A" has said; but away with frivolity and thoughtlessness.

(10) When the Church speaks generally to the larger political body, she should impress upon the atomic power states the necessity of order and peace and should advise the non-atomic power nations not to strive to obtain these means.

(11) Not everyone must do the same, but everyone must know what he does.4

What is encountered in these "theses" is an attempt to explicate a mandate for Christian action and guidance in the present awareness that no single action-program can completely express the Christian imperative for either the individual or the government in regard to war in the nuclear age. This can only result in a statement of differing responsibilities and a concluding sentence that "not everyone must do the same" even though everyone who calls himself a Christian is under obligation to act as befits a maker of peace.

Those who speak for nuclear realism see in the conflict between East and West communism and the free world, a gigantic power struggle in which, if outward peace is to be preserved, some semi-balance of a balance of power must be brought continually into being and those things done in economic and military maneuvers which will maintain stability, to the end that law and order in the respective spheres can prevail.

In the present nuclear crisis statesmen are called upon by the Church to handle responsibility and intelligently the power which in this era of history has been thrust upon them. Recognizing that nuclear power may be used for good or ill--the bomb is viewed as not evil in itself, but its good or evil is regarded as dependent on its possessor and the use he makes of it--the nuclear realists urge governments to take those steps which ease conflict, to continue negotiation rather than consider open hostility, and to work toward controlled disarmament.

An insight into the values of the nuclear realists may be gained from Sidney Hook when he says: "Survival ⋯ is the summum bonum for Communism, whereas the West, buttressed in part by belief in immortality, whether as a myth or fact, has always maintained that there are certain values which are more important than life itself."5

Those who speak for nuclear pacifism see an all-out atomic war as the greater of the two evils (Communism is the other) now confronting the West. In the nuclear age, war no longer can serve as the final arbiter of conflict--the ultima ratio--but rather now exists as a social institution outmoded by its own phenomenal, technological success.6 Thus a once necessary phase of human political structure has become a demonic element which threatens the total enterprise. Discontinuity is the keynote of the era if genocide is to be prevented and civilization, even under Communism, is to be preserved for posterity. The nuclear bomb is considered evil in itself and its possession as well as its use is regarded as falling outside the bounds of what the Christian can allow.[7]

With these imperatives in mind, Christians are under obligation to testify to the State that past patterns of response to conflict need to be radically modified. The social, economic, and ideological elements of the present crisis are seen as primary, and the concept of Satyagraha, first expounded by Mahatma Gandhi, is seen as a possible alternative to the present arms race and military stalemate. The Church's task is not only to seek truth amid falsity, to seek reconciliation amid hostility, and to "feed the hungry," but also clearly and explicitly to renounce the nuclear weapons and all tools of mass destruction.

The political reasoning involved in both nuclear realism and nuclear pacifism is of primary importance and is instructive at this point in understanding the nature of the moral problem.

To the nuclear realists, the Communist threat is seen as a full-fledged aggressive empire, exploding in history in the vacuum of a declining

European czarist and colonial system. It encompasses a philosophy of life and has a dynamic aggressiveness to carry out its ideals and social system. Such aggressiveness can be best met, halted and overcome by firmness in policy, strength in moral character, and prudence in diplomacy.

Historic parallels are cited: The Greeks through prudence and military strength successfully checked the expanding Persian empire in the history-changing battles of Marathon and Salamis. The Carthaginians, lacking both insight and power, were annihilated by the Romans as the latter grew to dominate the Mediterranean. When the Mohammedans sought to continue their expansion into Gaul, the armies of the Franks turned them back at Tours. The same reasoning suggests that Hitler might not have gained unprecedented ascendancy in Europe before being stopped if the Allies had been better prepared. These historical antecedents would indicate the need for firmness in the contemporary clash.[8]

To the nuclear pacifists, the threat of nuclear annihilation demands new directions in politico-military thinking. The criticism of present international politics is based on the hypothesis that only final disaster can result from the ever more highly developed weaponry of military science on both sides of the Iron Curtain. It is argued that both the Soviet Union and the United States have shown lack of "good faith" since the Second World War. This refusal to trust each other has brought about the breakdown of disarmament negotiations and the increasing spiral of mistrust and fear.[9]

Although Communism is acknowledged to be a grave threat to the values of the West, American leaders are urged to take unilateral steps in a graduated program of disarmament. Willingness to take initiatives in new negotiations accompanied by relaxation of military tension is seen as crucial if nuclear war is to be averted.[10] The use of all types of nonviolent efforts is encouraged.

The two most frequently cited historical examples for a non-violent approach are the movements led by Mahatma Gandhi and Martin Luther King; in the former India gained her independence through the use of nonviolent measures and in the latter the Negroes in the South started a dramatic process to secure justice in the United States.

In both nuclear pacifism and nuclear realism, therefore, historic precedents are cited, and in each case there is a definite pattern of political reasoning. The nuclear pacifist position implies and often states that it is wrong even to possess the nuclear weapons; the nuclear realist position contends that under certain conditions <u>to use</u> the hydrogen bombs would be justified. Neither position can command acceptance by all Christians; it would not be right to abandon the bombs nor to affect their destructiveness. The paradox can be stated in one sentence: While the <u>possession</u> of the hydrogen bombs can be justified by the Christian; the <u>use</u> of the nuclear weapons can never be accepted.[11] This may sound like a paradox and it may be such in terms of trying to affect a workable policy at either the governmental or the individual level. But it is the nature of the tension that exists for the Christian ethic in the nuclear dilemma at the present time.[12]

Two threats are involved --- the threat of nuclear annihilation and the threat of the triumph of communism. According to the Christian ethic, Christians have an obligation to avert both. On the one hand, to be faithful to the demands of political office is to do all that is possible to uphold justice, freedom and brotherhood; on the other hand, to be faithful to the moral demand of law and order is to do all that is possible to avoid and prevent a nuclear holocaust. Our dilemma results from the appearance that it is impossible to be faithful to the one imperative without being unfaithful to the other.[13]

Rationale for the Paradox

Such an ethical paradox arises from and is inherent in the nuclear weapons. Its ramifications are to be seen in the dual threat to mankind and the consequent responsibilities of Christians as citizens of this world. The two threats are "Communism" and "annihilation"; the two responsibilities are the preservation of justice and the preservation of law and order. We will look at these in order.

The Communist threat is not only one of political domination or tyrannical enslavement. There is no doubt that exploitation of the world by the Soviet Union is an evil to be resisted, but the threat to the Biblical faith is more subtle than this. Helmut Thielicke has expressed it well when he writes:

"The choice is not primarily between communism and destruction; the basic issue is rather whether we must in principle recognize the right of the stronger.... The person who chooses unlimited power must recognize what his ultimate choice is: He has decided against the Noachite ordering of the world, in which uncontrolled unlimited power was to find its limit in opposing power, and in which the principle of world-preservation consisted precisely in the fact that limits were set and, if occasion arose, were enforced by the use of power."[14]

To bow to the Communist threat is to admit defeat to a meaning of life set in the framework of righteousness; it would be to accept in practice the unethical concept: Might makes right. If the choice were only between Communism and annihilation, it might be an act of faith to choose enslavement in the belief that history would bring changes from within the resulting political order. However, the choice also involves, as Thielick points out, the willingness to allow the "rule of power" to have its way.

This is not all; another argument may be added. For the West unilaterally to renounce reliance on the megaton weapons would not mean an end or cessation of the power conflict. It might well mean only that the power centers of the world would be shifted to Moscow and Beijing (and Paris) rather than continuing also in Washington and London. The assumption that unilateral renunciation of the H-bomb by the West would leave a monarchial government centering in Moscow is by no means assured either in the immediate future or especially the more distant future. Rather, the existence of several nuclear power centers might well remain--centering in Moscow, Beijing and Paris. Would it not be irresponsible to argue that Moscow and Beijing

114

could more responsibly handle nuclear power than could Washington and London? Do not Christians, where they have opportunity, have the obligation to use power responsibly rather than abdicate its use to others?[15]

It is a constant threat that the strategy of deterrence will erupt into nuclear war. According to most of the persons we have been quoting, whether nuclear realist or nuclear pacifist, an all-out nuclear war could never be justified by Christians. The nuclear realists stress the need for the megaton weapons as a "threat," but these weapons lose their effectiveness as a deterrent if there is no intention to use them. The possession of megaton weapons necessitates willingness to put them to use if their deterrent strength is to be realized.

"Nuclear parity functions as an instrument of peace, i.e., as a deterrent against these weapons ever being used, only if and so long as you succeed in convincing your opponent that you are fully resolved to wage nuclear war if and when, in your opinion, the necessity for it arises •••• The stark and naked truth is indeed that to be effective deterrence depends on the threat of mutual annihilation."[16]

But for the Christian, as we have indicated, the crucial argument against the possession of the megaton weapons, even as a deterrent, is the recognition that he might be pressed to use them in a general attack on the enemy country. To engage in an all-out war with megaton weapons would be to bring on the chaos we are seeking to avert and, what is worse, would be to make us mass murderers on an unprecedented scale.

In so far as the State is ordained of God, heads of state are charged with the responsibility to uphold justice and promote the well-being of the community. It is the responsibility of the Church to provide those spiritual resources whereby government leaders may see beyond the temporal to the eternal source and norm of their strength and wisdom. Each age carries its own unique opportunities and duties.

The secular historical perspective today reveals the need for world-wide social, economic and political inter-relationships. The historic epoch in which we live is witnessing the birth-pangs of "world-civilization," an international ethos and regional consciousness; the death of purely nationalistic interests seems decreed by the movement of events. Concern for racial equality, international law, and scientific solidarity add to the "one-world" outlook which struggles to supersede the older and more provincial viewpoints. This is taking place "along-side" and "underneath" the more specific nuclear dilemma. Despite the strong movements opposing such a development in history (isolationists want to protect the nationalistic values of the past, Communists want only a "communist international"), such a trend appears irreversible in the longer perspective of human history.

There is a real service which the Church can render to the world (its mission is to minister to the world) by helping in the birth of a new age in international relations. For the trend toward internationalism, while it exists, is not inevitable in the short run. There is also a real responsibility which the Church has to support the striving for justice, law, and order in the community--which today includes a decisive world-wide dimension. This "long pull" for international governmental institutions is more fundamental for the structures of society than the "short run" nuclear dilemma. Solving the problems of an "international law and order" would greatly reduce the dangers in the nuclear dilemma. The latter threatens to abort twentieth-century efforts at world-community organization. However, neither an uncontrolled arms race nor unilateral disarmament by the West will do away with the overhanging "chaos" of nuclear destruction.

The dual obligation of the Church in the world today is (1) to promote the efforts to obtain justice for all peoples and at the same time (2) to do those things that will maintain stability on an international level. These positive functions, involving a world-wide transforming process, need to be carried out in such a way that the threat of negation of the entire enterprise is avoided, and the threat of a Communist take-over is averted. The duty of the Church is to make men aware of the nature of the crisis and to give guidance in the development of disciplines that make solution possible.

In summary we can say that the "paradox" which exists in a moral response to the nuclear dilemma results from two concepts of obligation at tension with one another in any existential analysis. The "duty" stemming from the Christian obligations of traditional citizenship is <u>to possess</u> the megaton weapons as a deterrent against aggression, but this "duty" necessitates the intention to use the weapons if the deterrent is to be effective. On the other hand, the duty stemming from the Christian imperative to limit violence to "just war" is to <u>renounce</u> the megaton weapons which under no conceivable circumstances could be used for defense and protection.

If one starts by saying that we are justified in <u>possessing</u> the nuclear bombs, he must logically assert his willingness to <u>use</u> them. If one starts by saying that the <u>use</u> of the nuclear bombs could never be justified, he is logically led to renounce possession of them.

The paradox centers in the thermonuclear weapons themselves. The political context gives the ethical paradox credulity and practicality, but it is not the context itself which presents the dilemma. The dual needs of international relations (to avoid both the paradox centers in the thermonuclear bombs themselves. The political context gives the tyranny and annihilation) and the dual obligations of the statesmen (to provide both freedom and order) existed in the pre-atomic age as well as in the atomic age. It is the nuclear weapons that provide the new dimension.

ENDNOTES

1. The Era of Atomic Power. Report of a Commission appointed by the British Council of Churches, (London: S.C.M. Press, 1946), p. 53.

2. Ibid., p. 54.

3. Ibid., pp. 56-57

4. "Die Heidelberger Thesen zur Atomfrage", in Atomzeitalter und Frieden, herausgegeben von Gunter Howe (Witten Berlin: Verlag. 1959), pp. 504-511, passim. Translation mine.

5. Sidney Hook in "Western Values and Total War," A Round-table Discussion by Sidney Hook, H. Stuart Hughes,

Hans J. Morgenthau, and C. P. Snow, Commentary, 32 (October, 1961), 282.

6. Although not a nuclear pacifist, John Cogley writes: "What we must begin to reckon with, then, is the idea that technology has succeeded in doing what all the wit and piety of the moralists through the ages failed to do: it has utterly eliminated the logic of war. When that fact really sinks in, war may disappear from the face of the earth. See "A World without War," Worldview, 2 (June, 1959), 8.

7. Gordon Zahn writes that the nuclear weapons "by their very nature are destructive of areas and populaces." See "An Island Disappears," Catholic World, 177 (May, 1953), 108.

8. In the Berlin crisis in the fall of 1961, Louis J. Halle argued that a firm stand in Berlin was the lesser risk for the West to take; see "Beyond This Crisis," The New Republic, 145 (October 2, 1961). 41-44.

9. "Your arguments finally reduce to the absolute necessity of breaking the circle, the vicious circle, of mutual distrust between us and the Soviet Union, and doing it fast, and arriving at what amounts to an American-Soviet alliance for the preservation of the peace and the denial of nuclear weapons to other nations. And I would maintain that the only way that circle can be broken and broken fast is by a dramatic act of renunciation on one side or the other." H. Stuart Hughes in "Western Values and Total War," op. cit., 292.

10. The show of strength in the Berlin Crisis in the fall of 1961 was regarded by nuclear pacifists, as worsening the crisis; making Berlin a city under the control of the, United Nations was advocated as an alternate policy. See Melvin J. Lasky, "Moving the U.N. to Berlin is not Utopian," New Republic, 145 (October 30, 1961). 9.

11. "It is the most paradoxical effect of nuclear penetrability that the weapon is successful only as long as it remains an unused threat; used, it means deadly failure." John H. Herz, "International Politics and Nuclear Dilemma," Nuclear Weapons and the Conflict of Conscience, edited by John C. Bennett (New York: Charles Scribner's Sons, 1962), p. 32.

12. The paradoxes are in the things themselves, and it is therefore not surprising that they are reflected in attitudes and policies." John H. Herz, op. cit., p. 32.

13. "We must insist that morality is relevant even in a thermonuclear age. While resisting enslavement by an inhuman social order, we must insist on using means that are not themselves inhuman and unjust. We must keep the world from being swallowed by the Communists, but we must keep the world from destroying itself too." James O'Gara. "More on the Bomb," Commonweal, 78 (April 12, 1963), 66.

14. Helmut Thielicke, "The New Situation in the Atomic Age." Religion in Life, 30 (Summer, 1961) 382-383. Translated by Karl H. Hertz.

15. Its logic (nuclear pacifism) will hold only if there are just two nuclear powers. If I have one adversary, and he has only me as adversary, I can with some degree of confidence predict his reaction to what I do. But if there is a third party (not to mention four or five), my action becomes less determinative, and I can hardly predict at all what they will do to each other." Tom F. Driver, "The Nuclear Dilemma and the Mind of Tragedy," Christianity and Crisis, (November 27, 1961), 212.

16. Carl Mayer, "Moral Issues in the Nuclear Dilemma," Christianity and Crisis, 22 (March 19, 1962), 36-38.

THE ETHICAL ASPECTS OF LIMITED WAR

In the field of international relations, Christian ethicists have stressed the values of freedom and order. These are polar concepts, and are seen as deriving their meaning from the religious teachings of the Christian faith. Morally concerned persons ought to work for both meaningful freedom for individuals, and order and stability in the human community. Both the dignity of individuals and security for all are basic moral requirements for society. Any discussion of social justice involves us in a consideration of the well-being of all members of the community. Seeking social justice in the human community means both restraining human aggression and providing structures in the society for the fulfillment of purposes by the members of the society. It is within this larger conceptual framework that one may discuss the more specific factors that relate to the ethical aspects of limited war. Consider the concept itself: Why should persons in our era of history talk about "limited war"? Similarly, when is war right in the atomic era?

The intercontinental ballistic missiles armed with nuclear warheads have become both the symbol and the reality of an evolution in military science and strategy in the twentieth century. It is the development of this potentially vast destructive power in our nuclear arsenals that has resulted in the political, military, and ethical concepts of limited war. The fact that nuclear power has become available by our technology has changed man's thinking about war and peace as well as his thinking about available sources of energy to run an industrialized society.

The massive use of violent force in the Second World War was justified by most American churchmen, both Protestant and Roman Catholic. The Roman Catholics tended to argue from the just war tradition that the ends sought by the Allies were freedom and justice, and that armed force as a last resort was necessitated by the historical events brought on by the Nazi and Fascist zealots. Although not supporting every aspect of the war, nor "endorsing it as a holy war or crusade,"[1] Catholics generally saw the war as "a struggle between the established Christian order"[2] and the serious challenge to those values by Nazism and Fascism. Thus support for the war was clearly within the limitations of the just war tradition. While specific actions were challenged as immoral, the war itself was seen as a moral undertaking.

Protestants, following the arguments of Reinhold Niebuhr, regarded the situation in the 1940s as a choice between war and tyranny. War was the lesser evil; totalitarianism was the greater denial of good. It was better to engage in a destructive war than to allow Hitler's forces to go unchallenged and to accept a culture in which one's children would be taught that kicking and killing Jewish persons were acceptable behavior. Edward L. Long, in a recent book, characterizes the attitude as "agonized participation" - the feeling that while war can never be regarded as good, it nevertheless "may sometimes be necessary for the prevention of a greater evil."[3]

For most Americans, however, the Second World War was a justified response to naked aggression-by the Germans in Poland and by the Japanese in the Pacific. Fighting in the nation's defense in response to an aggressive enemy is, as documented by Robert Tucker,[4] the common denominator in American thinking to justify warfare. Our cultural temperament would have us resist involvement in open warfare until it is "forced" upon us, until we are the victim of an aggressive attack; then to pursue the war until military victory is achieved is regarded as the only honorable path to follow.

Those who had justified large-scale war in the 1940s for the above reasons have argued in this decade, dramatically and forcefully, that an all-out nuclear war could never achieve any of the objectives which earlier had made violent force a legitimate tool of international politics. Such warfare was not a tool to be used to secure freedom, or order, or social justice.

They argued that: (1) an all-out nuclear war would not defend any nation, but would result in a mutual annihilation; (2) no one could claim that a nuclear war was the lesser evil; or that in some way it would achieve a greater good; (3) the very basis of law and order, justice, and freedom would be destroyed; that is, the human values sought would be lost in the very action taken to realize them; and (4) nonnuclear powers which might not even be a party to the conflict could easily be devastated in any war between the nuclear powers. The innocent would die with the guilty, and man's civilization itself would be threatened with extinction. Although this position, the nuclear pacifist position, is widely held by Christians in many denominations and countries, the contrasting arguments of the nuclear realists hold the allegiance of the majority of Christians concerned about international affairs. Those nuclear realist viewpoints deserve brief mention.

First, if an all-out nuclear war should be avoided, so also should we avoid a world-wide Communist tyranny. If it were a simple choice between "red" and "dead," Christians and morally sensitive persons still might not agree on what the choice should be, but it is not such a simple choice. There is another major alternative: the route of responsible statesmanship is to avoid *both* nuclear war and Communist tyranny-and as long as that alternative is possible, it is the desired goal and the objective to be pursued in the foreign policy of the free world.

Second, while all-out *use* of the nuclear weapons may be ethically unacceptable, it is not unacceptable to possess the weapons as a threat against their use by the other side. Such a distinction led a theologian like Paul Tillich to conclude that the first use of nuclear weapons could never be justified, but "their limited and selective use in response to a nuclear attack to prevent further use of the weapons could be justified."[5] Possession as a threat is acceptable; or to put it in another perspective, knowledge by the enemy that we have the capacity for retaliation forms the new reality or umbrella within which political decisions are now made.

Finally, the threat of annihilation is mutual. Thus the balance of power is still a political reality in today's world. Its contemporary form is deterrent strategy. To abdicate power because of its new dimension is to move out of the arena of responsible citizenship. The responsible use of power, not its misuse or renunciation, forms the basis for ethical action. The moral demand is for responsible, informed, and wise use of power in international affairs. Deterrent strategy is the modern version of that ancient Noachic covenant: "Whoever sheds the blood of man, by man shall his blood he shed."[6] Order rests upon restraint; or, theologically, man is made in God's image, and murder-unjustified and illegal killing—is wrong.

It is necessary to recount these arguments because the responsible use of armed force in international affairs is being challenged from two sides in our time. From the one side, there are those who argue that modern military science has changed everything. Violent force is anachronistic. Only the way of Gandhian nonviolence (or passive resistance) is ethically acceptable. There is no rational use for possession of modern weapons, no use that can be justified on the basis of moral argument. Martin Luther King's techniques of nonviolence are valid not only in the civil rights movement, but also in the international arena.

Other ethicists argue, however, that what is ruled out is not conflict, but the use of unlimited power which would destroy that which its possession protects. In the nuclear age men must learn to possess but not to use atomic weapons-that is the discipline needed to maintain international security. Louis J. Halle has pointed out that rattlesnakes do not use their deadly venom against their own species. While their limited power is used in combat, their unlimited power is not used. Rattlesnakes and other animals may use unlimited power outside their species, but they use limited power when fighting each other. Halle argues that such a law of nature must be applied by men to their warfare, and must become an established habit. "While all-out conflict may he consonant with limited weapons, absolute weapons require that conflict be limited."[7] Man must learn—it is not instinctive—not to use unlimited power in combat. We must distinguish between all-out suicidal war, which is not inevitable, and organized resistance to injustice which, given the nature of human history, most probably is a continuing component of our life on this planet.

On the other side are those who argue that modern military science has changed nothing. They see only continuity in history, and give little emphasis to discontinuity. In light of the nuclear weapons, they argue, man's political problems are intensified, but they are not basically changed. The fate of the atomic bombs will be the same as the fate of the crossbow; although the medieval Pope, Innocent II, in 1139 condemned the weapon as too barbaric for use in warfare, the crossbow was used.[8] The resolution by religious authorities of the day meant very little; strategists of the day could not allow their armies to fight without using the weapons made available to them by the technology of the day.

But crossbows are not nuclear weapons, because while the crossbow may have appeared more horrible than other weapons of the day, it did not result in the destruction of that which it claimed to protect. One contemporary wit has cracked, "Atomic bombs come in three sizes: small, medium, and where did everyone go?" They did not say that of the crossbow.

While war is evil, selected participation has been regarded as morally justified. It is justified when violence is used to secure freedom and order or to establish social justice, but annihilation has not been regarded in modern times as a legitimate objective.

Several of our leading strategists[9] argued that the Dulles doctrine of massive retaliation left us too few options in foreign policy. If atomic bombs were to be used to offset the massive land armies of Russia and China, then we were left with a choice of nuclear war or surrender in Europe, and the same kind of choice in any major confrontation with China. So they argued that a significant build up in our conventional forces was needed to give us flexibility in military power and more options in our foreign policy decisions. John F. Kennedy and Robert McNamara were impressed by such arguments, and such efforts were made when they took office.

Paul Ramsey of Princeton was one of the few ethicists to applaud this expansion of our military might as having moral values as well as increasing the range of military and political choices. Ramsey appreciated the fact that we were not left in an all-or-nothing posture—that we were not relying on atomic weapons for situations where their power was all out of proportion to the nature of the tension and conflict.[10]

In other words, one's tools must be appropriate for the job, and in seeking for values of freedom and order, or social justice and security, different strategies are appropriate for different situations. Insofar as the concept of limited war is viewed as filling a gap between nuclear deterrent strategy and powerlessness to act in less critical situations and circumstances, it may, as a tactical option, allow the achievement of values related to social justice that would not be otherwise possible.

The fact of nuclear weapons has dramatically altered another great reality of the history of our era. Especially in the second half of the twentieth century, one cannot ignore the immense struggle between the Communist and the non-Communist world and, increasingly, the struggle within the

Communist world itself.

The nuclear weapons have forced a "balance of terror" as Winston Churchill called it. The co-existence of the super powers does not mean that deep differences do not continue between them with respect to aims and objectives in international relations and that this in turn rests upon contrasting values and philosophies. In an earlier well-known writing, an outstanding Christian ethicist characterized communism as half-truth and positive error.[11]

Although the first assembly of the World Council of Churches meeting in Amsterdam in 1948 gained publicity when it declared that both laissez-faire capitalism and communism fell short of the Kingdom of God, and although some Christians have minimized the differences between the quality of life manifested in the East and the West, many others are very much aware of what they regard as the terribly misguided idealism of communism that thinks it can create a new world by killing and imprisoning all who may not share the vision of a classless society, created through the dictatorship of the proletariat.

There are those who minimize the conflict

and others who would turn it into a holy crusade; and both would seem to be wrong. Karl Barth has stated that it is as difficult to be a Christian in the East as it is in the West. At the same time, there are those who see the matter as good vs. evil, the righteous vs. the wicked, and rule out any attempts at agreements because, they say, one cannot make bargains with the devil. They advocate annihilation or slavery for the enemy.

But to turn the conflict into some kind of holy war is to ignore that compromises have been made, that negotiations do take place, and that war has not occurred between Russia and the United States despite prophecies of doom. Although the Biblical tradition does not deny conflict, it also affirms the common humanity of all men, thus indicating that there are grounds for reconciliation as well as causes of violence in the human drama.

The ideological struggle poses the question: What structures in society best allow for the growth of individuals and the realization of community goals? To what degree shall economic, social, and political planning be administered from central governments with authoritarian and/or dictatorial powers; or, to what degree shall society be "open" with wide scale citizen participation?

Harold E. Fey wrote in *The Christian Century:* "When the United States insists that no people should be subjected to such a process (Viet Cong War of Liberation) it is not saying that the freedom of choice it seeks to preserve must be exercised to choose democracy. It is simply saying that it will not permit any group of persons to impose on South Vietnam a process of violence which if it succeeds, will impose on that country a form of government to which no alternative is possible. The question of whether the Viet Cong is nationalist or communist or a mixture of both is beside the point. The important question is what it will become."[12]

Although these two ideological systems, reflected in democratic governments and totalitarian regimes, have dominated the Cold War for the past two decades, this struggle must now be seen against a different backdrop of history. It has been more than fifty years since the Communists gained control of the revolution in Russia, and more than fifty years since the United States entered World War I to make the world safe for democracy. During that time another world had been coming into being; and it promises to dominate world politics for the foreseeable future.

It is the revolution in the Third World, in the Southern hemisphere, in Southern Asia, Africa, and Latin America. This revolution has been called "the revolution of rising expectations." It is the attempt on the part of emerging nations to industrialize, to combat poverty, to overcome illiteracy, and to become strong, viable nations. Some have euphemized the aspect of revolution by talking about "rapid social change," but however labeled, it is an attempt to enter the technological era in a generation or two rather than follow a course of action that required Western Europe and North America two centuries.

A leading economist of the country has indicated[13] that these yet-to-be modernized nations include one billion people; that 500 million have not seen the inside of a school building; that 10 percent of the population of Calcutta live their lives on the streets; and that in Latin America, 10 percent of the people own 90 percent of the land. Rapid social change will become imperative for survival in the twentieth century.

Attitudes of churchmen vary with respect to

the Third World. The church itself has become a world-wide fellowship, something the late Archbishop of Canterbury, William Temple, noted as the "great new fact of our time." There is a strong sense of identification with the numerous nations in the Third World that seek to become independent, viable countries and peoples. Unlike Europe and America, there does not exist in the Third World a history of economic growth, participation in government, and emphasis on the rights of the individual and the supremacy of law. The desire of many for rapid social change would seem to make conflict inevitable.

There are Christian ethicists who see this rapid social change as the key to understanding the role of the church. As John C. Bennett wrote twenty years ago, modern social Christianity is characterized by "the attempt to see the world from the point of view of oppressed or neglected classes and races."[14] For many, the role of the church is to give itself wholeheartedly to the support of this technological and social remolding of the world's dispossessed peoples.

In this context, violence is seen as a tool for urgently needed social changes, and violence is not seen as intrinsically more immoral than all forms of non-violence. Alan Geyer has written, "Reinhold Niebuhr shocked our fixations on law and order and our fears of anarchy and conflict by declaring; 'If a season of violence can establish a just social system and can create the possibilities of its preservation, there is no purely ethical ground upon which it can be ruled out.' Niebuhr insists, as did Abraham Lincoln, that violence, bitter as it may be, serves at times as an instrument of a higher justice and an ultimate reconciliation."[15]

Those critics of present foreign policy who speak out of this context frequently argue that in addition to the disproportionate number of civilian dead in South Vietnam, the United States has so acted that the forces of reaction have triumphed rather than the forces working for social change. Nowhere is this more evident than in the matter of land reform-a movement or a tool of change that Americans find difficult to understand unless perhaps seen in the context of our westward expansion when land was made available by the government and by the large railroad companies. Land reform would seem to be at the root of many of the problems in Southern Asia, Latin America, and some other parts of the

Third World. Then when the Saigon government has recaptured an area, taken the land from the peasants, returned it to French Landowners, and collected back taxes, Americans wonder whether the Spirit of '76 has disappeared completely from that for which we fight. At the same time, it must be recognized that the Communists may eventually also take the land from the peasants and make it into communes; and that does not appear to be an acceptable alternative. But it is this kind of action that leads to the charge that U.S. policy is designed to block rapid social change in the Third World and aids the cause of injustice rather than the forces of justice.

The other position of Christian ethicists also grows out of humanitarian concerns, but with an emphasis on the need for order as well as freedom, and the need to avoid anarchy and tyranny. One but needs to mention the Congo, the Sudan, and Nigeria to realize the tremendous suffering and chaos that have accompanied the attempts at self-government in these nations. The hundreds of thousands who have died in these countries alone, it is claimed, represent a far greater human tragedy than Vietnam or Czechoslovakia. Again, one has but to mention Indonesia, Algeria, Greece,

South Korea, and Ghana to realize that attempted take-overs by Communist forces have been averted, sometimes by the narrowest of margins and sometimes with great cost in human life. But it also recognized that values of human freedom would have been denied if the Communists had won as they did in China, Cuba, Tibet, and Eastern Europe. It is this desire to avoid chaos or violent civil war, and tyranny or dictatorial rule in the Third World that leads many Christians to believe that the United States has the strength and the resources to intervene in such a way that the forces of the free world are strengthened, rather than the forces of the communist world. It is clear that social change and social stability are in conflict and that the revolution of rising expectations and ideological struggles are inter-related. For Americans, both our religious traditions and our political heritage dictate our concern to free people from hunger, exploitation, illiteracy, disease, and ignorance; and, at the same time, America's political objectives include for future generations the recognition of human rights, and governments which are responsive to international law.

The impact of numerous international organizations since the turn of the century needs to be more generally recognized. The work especially of the League of Nations and the United Nations has permeated and influenced the lives of all on the globe, for these organizations are clearly the culminations and the symbolic representations of hundreds of international organizations with humanitarian concerns.

From this international ethos springs a "common law of mankind," and these international agreements, coupled with an increasing acceptance of scientific technology, racial equality, and world-wide communications, mean that this is an age in which recognition of international inter-relationships will increasingly become part of man's perspective. The twentieth anniversary of the United Nations' Universal Declaration of Human Rights in 1968 is a legacy not to be ignored.

Up to this point, attention has been given to answering the question: When is war right? In reply, objectives of social justice and community security, the development of nuclear deterrence, the ideological struggle, the revolution of rising expectations, and the growth of international agreements have been considered.

There is a second question: What is right in war today? In a recent book entitled, *The Violent Peace,* the authors describe some fifty violent conflicts on this globe since 1945. To name even some of these conflicts is to be reminded that if an "atomic peace," or *pax atomica,* prevails, it is not a peace that comes with the Messianic Age, or the realization of the Kingdom of God. Rather, in Biblical terms, it is still a world in which Adam and Eve have been driven from the Garden of Eden and Cain and Abel are involved in violence.

Certainly the issues are diverse: nationalism vs. tribalism, independence vs. continued reliance on leadership given by colonial powers, governments dedicated to reform vs. governments tied to vested interests, and enlightened political and social concepts vs. submission to despotism and superstition.

In the midst of all of this, two movements and two men of Asia stand out: the rebirth of modern India under the leadership of Mahatma Gandhi, with his philosophy of non-violence; and the Communist takeover in China under the leadership of Mao-Tse-Tung, with his tactics of guerrilla warfare. These movements, and especially the means chosen to bring them about, seem to be very far apart. And indeed they are; but they have one outstanding trait in common: the involvement of the common man. Neither method could have succeeded without the cooperation of the people. If the masses had not cooperated, both Gandhi's non-violent resistance and Mao's guerrilla warfare would have failed in accomplishing their objectives.

Mao's strategy called for the guerrilla fighters to sustain themselves in the countryside. His famous analogy compared his fighters in the countryside to fish in the water. The support of the peasants (the water) is essential for the effectiveness of the guerrilla fighters (the fish). Equally important was the necessity to keep political goals and education before both fighters and peasants. A part of each guerrilla unit's energy was to be devoted to political indoctrination. Each team was to include a member responsible for this phase of the program. One news report from the Associated Press, dated 6 August 1968, indicated that Viet Cong military troops numbered between 207,000 and 222,000; and political indoctrinators numbered between 75,000 and 85,000.

On reflection, one will recognize that the same kind of cooperation on the part of the people is absolutely essential to the tactics of non-violence. Without the masses, Gandhi could not have secured the independence of India. He fasted in order to educate and to provide time for study. The people needed to understand in order to be ready to act. In like manner, the civil rights movement under Martin Luther King's leadership relied upon the understanding and cooperation of the masses. The nightly meetings in the churches throughout the South were times for education, commitment, growth, and a study of tactics and techniques. Without such mass participation, the civil rights movement would have collapsed.

One could argue that this involvement of the masses had its beginnings with Napoleon's universal military conscription to raise his armies. Gandhi's and Mao's use of the masses represented the full-fledged expansion of that idea. In such conceptual understanding, all this tends to reduce the distinction between combatant and non-combatant, common in just war theory and in medieval thought. The classic distinction between soldier and civilian had to do with functions; soldiers were the arm of the power of injustice or justice. Today, the functions of civilians and the army are both essential in determining the outcome of conflict.

This involvement of the masses of people, in conventional and non-conventional warfare, in both non-violent and guerrilla tactics, is a dimension of modern international conflict that is more significant today than it has ever been. Our vocabulary reflects the change, as may be noted especially in the word genocide. Where genocide has been threatened, peoples who have perceived the threat have generally taken actions to avert the threat.

The atomic balance of terror forms one example: fear of annihilation restrains us; desire to survive motivated us to seek alternative courses of action. And reflection on this modern problem has led that Danish Scientist-Poet, Piet Hein, to offer the following pithy advice:

> *"The noble art of losing face*
> *may one day save the human race*
> *and turn into eternal merit what*
> *weaker minds would call*
> *disgrace."[16]*

Two specific techniques of warfare have

come under heavy fire in the Vietnam War, both related to those members of society traditionally regarded as non-combatant, that is, the civilians. First has been the policy of terrorism practiced by the Communist insurgents and guerrillas, i.e., the systematic killing and kidnapping of community leaders whose services give form to the social structure and whose functions are essential to maintaining the community. Such attacks are designed to cause the society to crumble into chaos and enable the Communists to takeover. Second, just as debatable has been the counter-insurgency strategy of depriving the fish (guerrillas) of their water (support of the countryside). The clearing of civilians from large areas of land to create fire-free zones, defoliating jungle and rice fields alike to deprive the enemy of both sanctuary and food, and bulldozing villages to the ground to deny the guerrillas of their underground strongholds support this strategy. But the creation of millions of refugees and the deaths of large numbers of civilians has brought severe criticism.

Paul Ramsey has raised the question, "Is counter-insurgency, like insurgency, bound to be warfare over people as a means of getting at the other's forces?"[17] Few

Christian writers would argue with the contention that the selective (and often non-selective) terrorism is inherently immoral, and is a plan that cannot be regarded as moral by reference to the social reforms which the insurgency claims to bring to the country.

Concerning counter-insurgency, there has been plenty of debate, although certainly the majority of Christian writers have also condemned it, especially in South Vietnam, because of the large number of civilian dead and immense human suffering. (The lack of doctors and hospitals, and the very meaningful tie of Vietnamese families to the soil where their ancestors are buried, are important dimensions for that situation.) It is especially the methods employed in counter-insurgency warfare, however, that are uppermost in the minds of many American Christian ethicists when they argue that the lesser evil in Vietnam would have been a state under the rule of Ho Chi Minh, and that the continuation of the war in Vietnam has been the greater evil, both in the immediate and the long-range consequences.

Today's strategies for warfare include the essential involvement of civilians in a war effort and the important role of civilians both in technological development and social change. Both serve to indicate that common people are being involved in warfare in a way that was not true of the past. Today education is important for both the actual fighting force and for those who provide the essential back-up support.

In this perspective, some comments about American attitudes towards war and peace may be made. Americans have tended to justify violence for defensive purposes or in response to aggression. Despite the fact that South Korea was not regarded as militarily necessary to America's Pacific defenses in 1950, the nation felt it was morally obligated to repel the North Korean invasion. Contrarily, despite the fact that some American leadership felt it necessary to start bombing North Vietnam supply and infiltration routes, these measures seemed psychologically unacceptable to the American people until the North Vietnamese had made an attack (very much disputed now) on American ships in the Gulf of Tonkin.

The country is very much divided over the relation between diplomatic and military efforts. For many, war and diplomacy are two separate entities. When you go to war, political considerations are left behind, and some say that there is no substitute for victory regardless of political considerations.

Limited war means the absence of nuclear weapons, that is, the use of limited means of warfare. It also means that a clear statement of objectives is a primary dimension of modern war. Victory means the achievement of one's objectives, and therefore it is important to know what those objectives are. In the Second World War, victory meant the unconditional surrender of the enemy governments. In Korea, victory for the United States Police Forces meant the repelling of aggression and the acceptance of the 38th parallel as a boundary between North and South Korea.

A lesson needed to be learned is that the real test of a military establishment is how it serves the country's foreign policy. Clausewitz's dictum is applicable: "War is the continuation of politics by other means." Political objectives and military power are inter-related. It does make sense that "peace talk" should continue while actual fighting also continues, as in Korea or currently in Vietnam.

The crucial question is the statement of political objectives, and the recognition that political goals may be restated and revised as circumstances change and more basic attitudes are recognized. In that context, we can accept negotiated settlements and compromised agreements, de-escalation as well as escalation.

In a nuclear age, and especially in modern war, the goals are necessarily limited. One does not seek the destruction of the enemy; but rather, as Polybius said, as quoted by General Maxwell D. Taylor, "It is not the purpose of war to annihilate those who provoke it, but to cause them to mend their ways."[18] Ironically, this maxim may be quoted by both sides in the wars that have been waged in the decade of the sixties. It would appear, therefore, that conflict and negotiation are, and ought to be, inseparable in limited warfare.

ENDNOTES

1. Ralph Luther Moellering, *Modern War and the American Churches* (New York: American Press, 1956), p. 53.

2. *Ibid.*, quoted from *America* (20 December 1941).

3. Edward LeRoy Long, Jr., *War and Conscience in*

America (Philadelphia: Westminster Press, 1968), p, 41.

4. Cf. Robert W. Tucker, *The Just War: A Study* in *Contemporary American Doctrine* (Baltimore: The John Hopkins Press, 1960).

5. Paul Tillich, "The Nuclear Dilemma—A Discussion," *Christianity and Crisis* 21 (13 November 1961): 204.

6. Genesis 9:6.

7. Louis J. Halle, "Is War Obsolete?" *The New Republic* 146 (2 April 1962): 13.

8. Bernard and Fawn Brodie, *From Crossbow to H-Bomb* (New York: Dell Publishing Co., 1962), p. 35.

9. For example, Henry A. Kissinger, *The Necessity of Choice* (New York: Harper and Brothers, 1961) and Maxwell D. Taylor, *The Uncertain Trumpet* (New York: Harper and Brothers, 1960).

10. Paul Ramsey, "Turn Toward Just War," *Worldview* 5 (July-August 1962): 8-13.

11. John C. Bennett, *Christianity and Communism Today* (New York: Association Press, 1960), p. 19.

12. *The Christian Century* 82 (1 September 1965): 1054.

13. Robert Heilbroner, Visiting Lecturer, Bridgewater College (Virginia), 9 October 1968.

14. John C. Bennett, Christian Ethics and Social Policy (New York: Charles Scribner's Sons, 1946), p. 2.

15.   Alan Geyer, "Moral Dilemmas in Revolutionary
      Warfare," Action 33   (September 1966)

16.   Piet Hein, Grooks (Cambridge, Mass.:
      The M.LT. Press, 1966), p. 37.

17.   Paul Ramsey, "Is Vietnam a Just War?"

      Dialog 6 (Winter 1967): 27.

18.   New York Times, 18 February 1966, p. 12.

Reprinted from Journal of Church and State 13 (Winter
1971): 113-27; used by permission.

The War in Nigeria

Professor Mambula is an ordained minister and leader in the Church of the Brethren in Nigeria. He is the Provost of the Theological College of Northern Nigeria. He has done a great service to his church and to the mother church in the United States by dealing with crucial questions that confront the churches in Nigeria. We in this country can help not only with our prayers and material aid for the churches, but also by grappling with the questions that Mambula poses to them and to us.

The churches in northern Nigeria (both Brethren and other denominations) face unprovoked attacks by Islamic terrorists that cry out for attention and response. The terrorists share the ideology of other Islamic terrorists around the world. They wish to establish a, "sharia state" and view anything "Western" as their enemy. They believe that violence is their religious duty in their fight to preserve a "pure" Islam.

Mambula suggests in the Preface of his book, "Are There Limits to Pacifism?" (c: 2009), that "the police, civil defense corps, and the armed forces of the state" have the first responsibility to stop the violence of the Muslim religious fanatics. Later in the book, he points out the weaknesses of such government activity, i.e., the government is weak, ineffective, and does not have the resources to confront the violence and chaos. Mambula places alongside the question of law and order, the principle that only love can break the spiral of violence that threatens northern Nigeria. But there is real tension between maintaining life and maintaining peaceful relationships in the larger community.

Mambula begins the book by giving a number of definitions of pacifism, and he traces the rise of pacifism as a political factor during and following World War I. He also considers the influences of the Anabaptists, the Mennonite doctrine of nonresistance, the Quaker repudiation of violence, the Jehovah's Witnesses refusal to bear arms, and the Gandhian doctrine of nonviolence (Satyagraha). He also traces the history of the Church of the Brethren. He affirms that the greatest support for "peace" now comes from the disaster relief work, the refugee resettlement program, and our service programs.

Mambula provides an exhaustive documentation of the teachings of Jesus and the Early Church that support the pacifist position. While many of these teachings are familiar, the sheer totality of the quotations is impressive of his scholarship and the wide base of support for a pacifist stance. He is not raising the question about the "limits of pacifism" because he is unacquainted with the scriptural reasons Christians give for their position! The question arises in face of widespread killings of pastors and church members and the burning of churches and church-related properties.

Church History

The Early Church in the Roman Empire faced a similar situation in North Africa in the fourth century. The Church had endured persecution in the early fourth century under the Emperor Diocetian. The Roman governor in North Africa had required Christians to hand over their Scriptures to avoid persecution. Many did so. After Constantine became Emperor, Christianity was recognized as a legal religion. Many who had turned over the Scriptures and even worshipped the pagan gods returned to the Church. Some of them became or continued as leaders - priests and bishops.

The church in Carthage, a city that was a large government and economic center along the coast of the Mediterranean, received a new bishop by the name of Caecilian. He was consecrated by someone whom many regarded as a "traitor," that *is,* someone numbered among those who had turned over the Scriptures to the Roman governor during the Diocletian persecutions. In turn, these "purists" consecrated

Donatus as bishop and claimed they were the true and faithful church.

Disagreements arose between the Caecilians and the Donatists. The "zealous," usually the lower social classes, wanted to maintain the "purity" of the church. They demanded that those who had been traitors not be allowed in any leadership position. Only the faithful during persecution should be so recognized. They became known as the "Circumcellions," a sub-group of the Donatists who followed Bishop Donatus. They insisted that the sacraments were valid only if performed by "faithful" priests.

They resorted to violence to make their demands. They killed the opposition indiscriminately. All sacraments not performed by faithful priests were invalid. The true church did not exist unless presided over by their priests.

The theologian, Saint Augustine, the most important intellectual of the day, said the church had a right to try to stop the violence of the religious fanatics. He did not advocate vigilante groups, nor did he advocate seeking vengeance. Rather, he said that the state, the official government, had the civic duty to fight for law and order and to control the terrorists. Augustine planted the seeds for "just war" thinking. The terrorists were slowed down, but they did not die out until the Arab conquest of north Africa in the 7th-8th century.

The Present Century

The book by Mambula is a daunting challenge to theologians in the Church of the Brethren. An opening illustration in the book by Rufus Bowman, "*The Church of the Brethren and War*", describes the massacre of some Brethren in Morrison's Cove in Pennsylvania in the eighteenth century. As they died, they said, "God wills it." I don't think we can recommend to the Brethren in northern Nigeria that their only response to the killings of members and pastors should be, "God wills it." They have a responsibility to work to stop the killing. The government of Nigeria has the first obligation to do so.

Mambula does an excellent job of describing how Christian groups, including the Brethren, are reaching out to Muslim communities to build bridges of understanding and lay the foundation of better relations. Those efforts will go a long way to improve relationships between the two religions and their people and institutions. However, if past history, both in the fourth century and the twentieth century, is a guide, these efforts will not persuade the fanatics and terrorists to stop. They believe that they must use violence to establish a pure "sharia" (Islamic law) government and or nation.

They remember the history of the Caliphate of the Ottoman Empire which came to an end following World War I. Ultimately, they would wish to re-establish such a world-wide state. In the process they know that the Church must be destroyed, and anything associated with Western civilization as well. There is no compromise. They are committed to killing their perceived enemies. Violence and terror are means to their end. Even genocide is part of their weaponry to establish a Muslim caliphate as is evident in Syria and Iraq. (Sept. 2014)

It is also true that the nature of warfare and conflict has changed in the new millennium. We used to be able to talk about nation states, declarations of war, and peace treaties. Today we confront endless conflict and warfare, and enemies that are networks of operatives that cross state boundaries. The base of operations may be in one country and the actual warfare in another country. Some of the networks of terrorists are connected; some operate as independent units in their own geographical area. There are Islamic terrorist groups in places as diverse as China, Indonesia, Thailand, various countries in Africa, and most of the countries in the Middle East.

Recent news reports (February, 2013) indicate that the United States is setting up a drone base in the country of Niger in Africa. (The country is north of Nigeria, east of Mali, and south of Libya and Algeria.) At the moment, the drones will be used for surveillance over Mali, primarily to aid the French there in their conflict with Al Qaeda terrorists. But in the future, the areas of drone activity could be expanded, and the drones could be armed and used to destroy specific targets as they have done in Pakistan and Yemen. It is not known if the Al Qaeda group in Mali has any connections with the Boko Haram group in Nigeria. They do have similar ideologies, and both are committed to the establishment of "sharia" states and governments.

The conflict in northern Africa in the time of Augustine lasted two hundred years. The Circumcellions, a subgroup of the Donatists, did not die out until the Arab conquest of North Africa in the seventh century. When Muslims gained the ascendancy, and Christianity died out, the conflict between the various Christian groups stopped. There is little or no indication that the Muslim jihadists will give up their fight any time soon anywhere in the world. Al Qaeda groups have failed to set up Islamic theocracies in Algeria and in Somalia. It remains to be seen if they will succeed in Nigeria.

Bibliography

Gonzalez, Justo L. THE STORY OF CHRISTIANITY. Volume I: The Early Church to the Dawn of the Reformation. Harper San Francisco: 1984.

Mambula, Musa A. ARE THERE LIMITS TO PACIFISM? THE NIGERIAN DILEMMA. Kaduna, Nigeria: Prudent Universal Press, 2009.

Rambo, Shelly. "Changing the Conversation: Theologizing War in the Twenty-First Century." THEOLOGY TODAY, 69, No. 4 (2013), 441- 462.

Weigel, George. FAITH, REASON, AND THE WAR AGAINST JIHADISM. New York: Doubleday, 2007.

Wikipedia: "Donatism."

Nuclear Pacifism vs. Nuclear Realism

This date, August 6th, 1945, is a part of my mental baggage. It was toward the end of World War II. I was between my sophomore and junior years of high school. It was the date of the bombing of Hiroshima. It was reported that 80,000 people had died. A second atomic bomb exploded over Nagasaki on August 9, 1945. It was reported that 60,000 people had died. Obliteration bombings were not new. In March, it was reported that 100,000 had died in Tokyo as the result of an obliteration fire-bombing of that city. And in February of 1945, it was reported that as many as 200,000 had died in an obliteration fire-bombing of Dresden, Germany. The city was full of refugees.

Japan surrendered to the Allies on August 14, 1945. My father drove the family to the town square of Troy, Ohio, to see the celebration. The square was a very large round-about intersection in the center of the town.

My father was a pastor in the Church of the Brethren. He was a pacifist. I learned that point of view. In my sophomore year in high school, I remember that I was the only one in my sophomore homeroom that did not buy war stamps. Instead I bought Brethren Service certificates. My education at home did two things for me: It gave me an interest in peace studies, and it gave me an interest in international relations. I went to Manchester College, now Manchester University, in Indiana. The college established the first program in peace studies in the nation. There are now over two hundred such programs. I was the first peace studies major at Manchester, and therefore the first in the nation.

It was brilliant program under the leadership of Dr. Gladdys Muir. But I also took a course in basic Christian theology from Dr. R. H. Miller which over the years proved to be more influential than the peace studies program. I graduated from college in 1951.

Nine years later, when I was doing my doctoral work at Boston University, my major professor in systematic theology was Dr. L. Harold DeWolf. He was a just war theologian in a School of Theology that was famous for having two of the most famous pacifists in the Methodist church. During the time that I was there, Dr. DeWolf preached a sermon, "Blind Samson or Christ." He said that a nuclear war could never meet the conditions laid down by just war theory. He said that the United States must unilaterally give up its nuclear weapons; it could never fight a just war with such weapons.

Just war theory includes seven criteria to justify a "just war." They include these three: there must be a reasonable hope for victory; the good to be achieved must outweigh the evil effects; and means proportionate to the ends must be used. DeWolf said that nuclear war could never meet those criteria.

Block-buster bombs used in WWII had the equivalent of two tons of TNT. The bomb that was dropped on Hiroshima was the equivalent of 20,000 tons of TNT. Several years later, on March 1, 1954, the United States exploded a hydrogen bomb in the Marshal Islands on the Bikini Atoll that was the equivalent of 20,000,000 tons of TNT. Several years after that, in 1958, the United States tested successfully an intercontinental missile that could travel thousands of miles in about 30 minutes. It was wedded to a nuclear warhead, and became known as an ICBM.

Eventually, American defense policy and Russian defense policy in the Cold War became known as "Mutual Assured Destruction," or short, simply as M-A-D, "MAD." Both countries developed what was commonly referred to as the "nuclear triad." There were three types of the nuclear weapons: missiles in silos based around the country; missiles in long-range bombers kept in the air twenty-four hours a day; and missiles in submarines that patrolled the oceans of the world. In other words, it was understood by both sides in the Cold War that if you attack us with nuclear weapons, you can be assured that we will retaliate, and both civilizations will be destroyed.

In the winter and spring of 1959-1960, I was ready to select a topic for my doctoral dissertation. I proposed to Dr. Harold DeWolf that I do a dissertation on the topic, "A Theological Evaluation of Nuclear Pacifism." He approved. I later found out that the Dean of the School, a pacifist, and the leading social ethicist of the School, another pacifist, thought that the concept lacked coherence and integrity and would never fly.

I worked on the dissertation during the next year and a half, and turned in my copy of it in August, 1961, the week before I left to come to Bridgewater College. I had concluded the paper by summarizing and quoting a study by the Heidelberg Commission of the German Lutheran Church saying that some Christians in the church and in the government must say "yes" to nuclear weapons, and some must say "no."

Two months after I had been teaching at Bridgewater, I received a letter from Dr. DeWolf. The letter said that I had a good dissertation, but it wasn't finished yet. The dissertation lacked an adequate conclusion, it lacked sufficient analysis, and it needed to identify the watersheds of the arguments set forth in the manuscript.   In short, it did not meet the standards that had been established by the University for all dissertations.

In the months that followed, I set about to make the corrections. I returned to Boston University in the two summers that followed to use the excellent libraries in the Boston area. Here at home, I used the libraries at the University of Virginia, Catholic University in D.C., and the Library of Congress. By the next year, my first reader, Dr. DeWolf, had gone on Sabbatical to Africa. My second reader, Dr. S. Paul Schilling, became my first reader. Dr. Nils Ehrenstrom became my second reader. Dr. Schilling said I had to have acceptable criteria to evaluate the arguments.   My second reader suggested that I completely rewrite the first chapter, and go on from there.   Five   years   passed.   I   had   a completely new dissertation – literally.

Footnote: When I retired from teaching at Bridgewater College, I took the first so-called dissertation, paginated it, made copies, had it bound, and titled it, *The Origins of Nuclear Pacifism.* I took the completed dissertation, a carbon copy, had it bound, and titled it, *Nuclear Pacifism vs. Nuclear Realism.*   The title, An Evaluation of Nuclear Pacifism, was no longer needed in my opinion.

Basically, nuclear pacifists are those just war theologians who called for unilateral nuclear disarmament. The ethical argument centered around two questions: Is it ever just to use nuclear weapons? And, two, Is it just to possess nuclear weapons? If three conditions of just war could never be met in a nuclear war: no victory possible, the good could not outweigh the evil, and more innocents would be destroyed than protected.... Then how could the use of the weapons ever be justified? If it is not just to use the weapons, what could justify possessing them?

The questions were debated at the World Council of Churches assembly meeting in New Delhi, India in 1961. The same questions were debated at the Roman Catholic Second Vatican Council meeting in Rome in 1962. By majority votes, both bodies approved statements that said the Church could accept the possession of nuclear weapons for deterrent purposes, but could not approve their use in a nuclear war.

In 1962, I remember being on a plane flight from Dulles in DC to O'Hare in Chicago. My seat mate was a Roman Catholic business man from Milwaukee, Wisconsin. I remember telling him at the time that Vatican II was debating the nuclear questions at the time, and asking what he thought. He was unaware that the item was on the agenda of Vatican II. But he told me, every

166

night the Roman Catholics in his community tuned in the radio to find out if Vatican II had said anything new about birth control that day!! (After all, what is most important?)

Criteria for evaluating the arguments were necessary. Four norms were established: (1) The Kingdom of God and History, (2) Love and Justice, (3) The Responsible Society (a concept taken from World Council of Churches study commissions), and (4) The Calculation of Consequences. These criteria were applied to the specific arguments, to the motifs, and to the theological perspectives. As you might imagine, that made for a much longer dissertation than the original.

The nuclear pacifists were characterized as those who said, "Better Red than Dead." The nationalists were those who were characterized as saying, "Better Dead than Red." The nuclear realists were those who were characterized as saying "Better neither Dead nor Red." That is a simplification of the arguments.

As usual at the Boston University School of Theology, the entire faculty was invited to the oral defense of the dissertation. That was in the spring of 1966. Twelve members of the faculty showed up. Each was allotted ten minutes to ask questions. My two readers were on different sides of the question, and they did not press me or each other. One faculty member wanted to know what the Japanese theologians thought about the issue. (There were and are many Christians in Japan; in fact the largest community of Christians in 1945 was in Nagasaki.) I said that I had not evaluated those theologians and did not know the answer. Three faculty members that were opposed to my project and opposed to the conclusions did not show up. (DeWolf, Muelder, Deats) Thus I was saved from their "veto" votes.

I went to the Boston University Commencement that spring, got my "union card," and continued to teach at Bridgewater College with a small increase in salary the next year.

Two footnotes: (1) A friend, Dr. James Stayer, Queens College, University of Ontario, Canada, sent me a note at the end of the Cold War. He noted that the bet or the gamble of "Neither Red nor Dead" had paid off; we had not all died, nor had we unilaterally disarmed.

(2) At one time we had 31,000 nuclear weapons in our arsenal. Now we have about 5,000. How many do we need in the 21st century? They are very expensive to maintain, modernize, and keep ready to use. They are still in missile silos, on B-52 long-range bombers, and in nuclear submarines patrolling the seven seas. The Cold War has been over for a long time. The Cold War

lasted from 1947 to 1991. It has been over for 22 years. The nuclear weapons are not the best weapons for fighting terrorists!! It is very expensive to keep them, modernize them, and pay for the costs of cleaning up nuclear waste, et cetera. How about accidents?

(This presentation was delivered as a talk at Rotary Club, Bridgewater, VA on August 6, 2013. The origin and basis of the talk was a Dissertation.)

Nuclear Pacifism/Nuclear Realism

Appendix

Arguments of the nuclear pacifists:

1. Possession of the nuclear weapons indicates the willingness to use the weapons under certain circumstances. Thus the crucial question for consideration must be the rightness or the wrongness of the <u>use</u> of these weapons, for continued possession will surely result in their being used sometime somewhere regardless of present stated intentions. But their use can never be justified.

2. The quantitative increase in destructive energy has brought about a qualitative change in the ethical decisions with respect to just warfare.

Atomic power represented a 20,000-fold increase in destructive power; hydrogen weapons represented a 20,000,000-fold increase in power. Such weapons can never be used justifiably; they are <u>in themselves</u> an evil to be avoided.

Furthermore . . .

3. They represent the possible end of man's civilizations. A total all-out nuclear war would mean the end of society as we know it, the mutual annihilation of the United States and the Soviet Union, and the possible destruction of all other major centers of technology and culture.

4. The Christian can never regard nuclear war as just warfare because:
  - the innocent as well as the guilty are deliberately killed,
  - the resulting evil would far outweigh any good that one could hope to accomplish, and
  - in nuclear war there is no reasonable hope of victory.

While these considerations should prove decisive, there are those who believe that there is another important traditional consideration.

5. A just war must have a just cause, but in the conflict between East and West, both "capitalism" and "communism" stand under judgment. Both systems fall far short of Christian principles—one system because it denies political freedom and tolerance of minorities, the other because it encourages waste and too frequently results in no economic

security. According to Karl Barth, the "climates" of the two systems are such that it is as difficult to be a Christian in the West as in the East. To fight for either side in the name of Christian love and justice is a misnomer. In addition, "massive retaliation" is certainly an evil cause.

6. It is assumed in these circles that the arms race has an inevitable end--- cataclysmic nuclear war. C.P. Snow: We know that some of these bombs are going to explode in the next ten years. Others: The end of the arms race is war.

Even if not, our sensitivity to ethical values is being destroyed.

Arguments of the nuclear realists:

1. Possession of the nuclear weapons is necessary in the modern world, to secure justice, to maintain law and order rather than chaos; the weapons are "given"--- to deny them is to attempt to go back to an earlier period of history, to be 'reactionary'; to engage in wishful-thinking.

2. There has been a change, to be sure, but the analysis of the change is crucial. What is needed is an understanding and use of deterrence strategy, not unilateral disarmament.

Military strategy has drastically changed—making threats "credible" to the enemy, developing 'second strike' capacity, and recognizing the change in space and time of the nuclear weapons is essential.

3. The slogans, "better dead than red" or "better red than dead" are not the only possibilities; as long as there is an alternative: BETTER NEITHER DEAD NOR RED, that is the responsible course of action to follow.

4. One needs to ask not what the specific criteria are with respect to just war, but rather ask about the values represented in that tradition. What is needed is a new DISCIPLINE. We must learn to possess the weapons, but not use them in mortal combat. Like the rattlesnakes, we have now unlimited power in terms of our own species: to use it would be suicide for all concerned. Unlike the rattlesnake, we do not act from instinct; rather we must acquire a discipline, a learning, a new method, and a new habit.

5. There are profound differences in the cultural values represented in the "East" and the "West" _ . a history of totalitarianism on one hand, and a history of parliaments and democratic processes on the other hand. Although the church as the church might face problems in either culture,

there are cultural values that are derivative that merit support, and are more than just preferences--- they are life and death values.

6. Every age of transition produces chaos, as well as new values; what is called for is clear thinking, a discriminating spirit, and keen analysis.

> (From work on my dissertation, used in classes and presentations)

Made in the USA
Charleston, SC
14 February 2015